STUDIES

This series, specially c

Society, provides a guide to the current interpretations of the
key themes of economic and social history in which advances
have recently been made or in which there has been significant
debate.

Originally entitled 'Studies in Economic History', in 1974
the series had its scope extended to include topics on social
history, and the new series title, 'Studies in Economic and
Social History', signals this development.

The series gives readers access to the best work done, helps
them to draw their own conclusions in major fields of study,
and by means of the critical bibliography in each book guides
them in the selection of further reading. The aim is to provide
a springboard to further work rather than a set of pre-
packaged conclusions or short-cuts.

ECONOMIC HISTORY SOCIETY

The Economic History Society, which numbers around 3000
members, publishes the *Economic History Review* four times a
(free to members) and holds an annual conference.
Inquiries about membership should be addressed to the
Assistant Secretary, Economic History Society, PO Box 190, 1
Grenville Road, Cambridge CB1 3QG. Full-time students may
join at special rates.

STUDIES IN ECONOMIC AND SOCIAL HISTORY

Edited for the Economic Society by L.A. Clarkson

PUBLISHED TITLES INCLUDE

Published titles continued overleaf

OTHER TITLES IN PREPARATION

The Population of Britain in the Nineteenth Century

Prepared for
The Economic History Society by

ROBERT WOODS

Professor of Geography
and Director of the Graduate Programme
in Population Studies,
University of Liverpool

M

First published in 1992 by
MACMILLAN EDUCATION LTD
Houndmills, Basingstoke, Hampshire RG21 2XS
and London
Companies and representatives
throughout the world

ISBN 0–333–51882–9

A catalogue record for this book is available
from the British Library.

Printed in Hong Kong

Series Standing Order

If you would like to receive future titles in this series as they are published, you can make use of our standing order facility. To place a standing order please contact your bookseller or, in case of difficulty, write to us at the address below with your name and address and the name of the series. Please state with which title you wish to begin your standing order. (If you live outside the United Kingdom we may not have the rights for your area, in which case we will forward your order to the publisher concerned.)

Customer Services Department, Macmillan Distribution Ltd
Houndmills, Basingstoke, Hampshire, RG21 2XS, England.

Contents

List of Figures

List of Tables

Editor's Preface

When this series was established in 1968 the first editor, the late Professor M.W. Flinn, laid down three guiding principles. The books should be concerned with important fields of economic history; they should be surveys of the current state of scholarship rather than a vehicle for the specialist views of the authors; and, above all, they were to be introductions to their subject and not 'a set of pre-packaged conclusions'. These aims were admirably fulfilled by Professor Flinn and by his successor, Professor T.C. Smout, who took over the series in 1977. As it passes to its third editor and approaches its third decade, the principles remain the same.

Nevertheless, times change, even though principles do not. The series was launched when the study of economic history was burgeoning and new findings and fresh interpretations were threatening to overwhelm students – and sometimes their teachers. The series has expanded its scope, particularly in the area of social history – although the distinction between 'economic' and 'social' is sometimes hard to recognise and even more difficult to sustain. It has also extended geographically; its roots remain firmly British, but an increasing number of titles is concerned with the economic and social history of the wider world. However, some of the early titles can no longer claim to be introductions to the current state of scholarship; and the discipline as a whole lacks the heady growth of the 1960s and early 1970s. To overcome the first problem a number of new editions, or entirely new works, have been commissioned – some have already appeared. To deal with the second, the aim remains to publish up-to-date introductions to important areas of debate. If the series can demonstrate to students and their teachers the importance of the discipline of economic and social history and excite its further study, it will continue the task so ably begun by its first two editors.

L. A. CLARKSON
Editor

Author's Preface

This is a study in historical demography written by a geographer. It focuses on the form and nature of long-term population change in Great Britain, but it does so, where necessary, by stressing the geographical variability of demographic forms and the role of population re-distribution. Demography is a technical subject which is inherently quantitative and rather empirical in outlook. It often rests uneasily with social theory and social history, but without the detailed evaluation, description and analysis of population statistics which demography provides, one cannot hope even to begin to understand the causes and consequences of the rise of Victorian cities, the wider significance of marriage, family planning and the sanitary revolution. This pamphlet has been written for economic and social historians in a way that should prove accessible, but it does introduce demographic indices as descriptive devices, hence the brief *Glossary of Demographic Terms*, and it does dwell on the changing nature of that shifting sand created by official statistics. It is, therefore, not only a brief introduction to a body of literature, but also an opinionated guide to certain fundamental research questions to which that literature relates either explicitly or implicitly. Most of these questions remain only partially answered, the victims of inadequate data or unsophisticated theories, but herein lies the interest and the challenge.

I should like to express my thanks to those historical demographers who have provided help, support and advice on matters associated with the population of Britain in the nineteenth century, but especially Gerry Kearns, Paul Laxton, Graham Mooney, Naomi Williams, Sally Sheard, Chris Smith, Andy Hinde, Eilidh Garrett, Patti Watterson, John Woodward, Dick Lawton, Chris Wilson and Michael Anderson. Finally, I owe a special debt to Alison, Rachel and Gavin.

May Day 1991

1 Malthus's Britain

When, in 1803, Malthus completed his chapters on England, Scotland and Ireland for the much enlarged second edition of *An Essay on the Principle of Population* (Malthus, 1803) he was able to create a picture of great variety in terms of form and shade. In England the checks to population were much affected by social class, the opportunities for employment and the physical environment. The restraint on marriage which led to high levels of celibacy and a substantial gap between age at sexual maturity and age at marriage was most obvious among sons of tradesmen and farmers, clerks in counting houses and servants who lived with the families of the rich. Even 'those among the higher classes, who live principally in towns, often want the inclination to marry, from the facility with which they can indulge themselves in an illicit intercourse with the sex'. This self-imposed restraint on marriage operated with 'considerable force throughout all the classes of the community'.

Malthus was also clear in the way he depicted the level of mortality in England and especially the manner in which it varied with the extent of urbanization. Using what we would now call a mortality ratio or the crude death rate (CDR), he showed that while the great towns had CDRs per thousand population from 44 to 53, 'moderate' towns had 36 to 42 and 'country villages' only 22 to 25.

> There certainly seems to be something in great towns, and even moderate towns, peculiarly unfavourable to the very early stages of life; and the part of the community on which the mortality principally falls, seems to indicate that it arises more from the closeness and foulness of the air, which may be supposed to be unfavourable to the tender lungs of children, and the greater confinement which they almost necessarily experience, than from the superior degree of

13

luxury and debauchery usually and justly attributed to towns. A married pair with the best constitutions, who lead the most regular and quiet life, seldom find that their children enjoy the same health in towns as in the country. (Malthus, 1803, *256–7*)

Since great cities and manufacturing centres were growing rapidly in the late eighteenth century it was clear to Malthus that the void created by excessive urban mortality had to be filled by 'a constant supply of recruits flowing in from the redundant births of the country'. Aspects similar to the English scene were also to be found in Scotland, although the contrast was probably even sharper. For example, in rural Scotland:

those parishes where manufacturers have been introduced, which afforded employment to children as soon as they have reached their 6th or 7th year, a habit of marrying early naturally follows; and while the manufacture continues to flourish and increase, the evil arising from it is not very perceptible; though humanity must confess with a sigh that one of the reasons why it is not so perceptible is that room is made for fresh families by the unnatural mortality which takes place among the children so employed. (Malthus, 1803, *283*)

Malthus found examples of the excessive subdivision of land holdings and landlord exploitation in the Highlands and Islands. Observations were also made on how prolific Scottish women were; the advantages of the Scottish system of voluntary poor relief which obliged the common people to be self-reliant, to care for relatives in sickness and old age and only to turn to the parish 'as a last resource in cases of extreme distress'; and that 'half the surplus of births was drawn off in emigration'. 'Scotland is certainly still over-peopled, but not so much as it was a century or half a century ago, when it contained fewer inhabitants'.

On Ireland, Malthus was also quite clear.

The details of the population of Ireland are but little known. I shall only observe, therefore, that the extended use of potatoes has allowed of a very rapid increase of it during the last century. But the cheapness of this nourishing root, and the small piece of ground which, under this kind of cultivation, will in average years produce the food for a family, joined to the ignorance and barbarism of the people, which have prompted them to follow their inclinations with no other prospect than an immediate bare subsistence, have encouraged marriage to such a degree that the population is pushed much beyond the industry and present resources of the country; and the consequence naturally is, that the lower classes of people are in the most depressed and miserable state. The checks to the population are of course chiefly of the positive kind, and arise from the diseases occasioned by squalid poverty, by damp and wretched cabins, by bad and insufficient clothing, by the filth of their persons, and occasional want. To these positive checks have, of late years, been added the vice and misery of intestine commotion, of civil war, and of martial law. (Malthus, 1803, *291–2*)

There are several good reasons for allowing Thomas Robert Malthus (1766–1834) to introduce us to the population of Britain in the early nineteenth century, some of which will already be apparent. Malthus was an extremely shrewd and, by 1803, well-informed observer of his times. He was also able to combine a facility for statistical analysis with a reading of the considerable literature available to him drawn from the work of fellow political economists. But Malthus was much more than a commentator. His primary intention in the first edition of *An Essay on the Principle of Population*, published anonymously in 1798, had been to demonstrate the imperfectability of human kind consequent upon society's inability to rid itself of misery and vice. These two sentinels at the cemetery gate were themselves, in his view, the direct consequences of population's ability to grow at a rate that followed a geometrical progression while food supplies could only be expanded at an arithmetical rate.

For illustrative purposes Malthus applied Benjamin Franklin's calculations on the rate of population growth of the United States – doubling every twenty-five years – to his own estimate of the current population of 'this Island', seven millions (Malthus, 1798, *74*). Malthus chose the United States because it provided an example of relatively unchecked population growth. After fifty years of such geometrical increase Britain's population would be 28 millions and after a century, 112 millions. But even assuming that agricultural production could support those initial seven millions, in fifty and one hundred years it would only be able to cope with 21 and 35 millions, leaving at least seven and seventy-seven millions, respectively, 'totally unprovided for', the victims of misery and vice, starvation and disease, or future emigrants.

This natural inequality of the two powers of population and production in the earth, and that great law of our nature which must constantly keep their effects equal, from the great difficulty that to me appears insurmountable in the way to perfectability of society. All other arguments are of slight and subordinate consideration in comparison of this. I see no way by which man can escape from the weight of this law which pervades all animated nature. (Malthus, 1798, *72*).

Let us set aside the question of Malthus's logic and the manner in which he derived the geometrical and arithmetical series, and turn to that aspect of the *Principle of Population* which became most significant in the second and subsequent editions, namely the checks to population growth. Although the ultimate check to population appeared to be want of food arising from the different ratios according to which population and food supplies increase, the immediate checks 'are all resolvable into moral restraint, vice and misery' (Malthus, 1803, *18*). Of these, the 'positive checks', as Malthus called them, included 'all unwholesome occupations, severe labour and exposure to the seasons, extreme poverty, bad nursing of children, great towns, excesses of all kinds, the whole train of common diseases and epidemics, wars, plague, and famine'. The preventive checks could largely be equated with 'restraint from marriage which is not followed by irregular gratifications', while 'promiscuous intercourse, unnatural passions, violations of the marriage bed, and improper arts to conceal the consequences of irregular connections, are preventive checks that clearly come under the head of vice'.

16

Having outlined the reasons for their existence and described their principal characteristics Malthus proceeded to document their workings in a wide range of societies, including England, Scotland and Ireland. But before doing so he also made what proved to be another telling observation in the 1806 edition of his essay: the positive and preventive checks will tend to be inversely related. In countries with high mortality, the preventive check will not be prominent while in those that are naturally healthy, where mortality is low, the preventive check will be found to prevail with considerable force.

When, finally, Malthus did turn to discuss the population of Great Britain and Ireland he found, as we have already seen, many illustrations of his principle. The preventive check was strong among all classes, but especially among farmers' sons and clerks; mortality was rather low, but not in the great cities, the manufacturing centres or among the lowest classes; and in Ireland, where the preventive check was weak, the situation was dire, or about to become so.

Without doubt, Malthus is Britain's most celebrated, but also controversial, demographer. In the nineteenth century, his works were at one of the same time an inspiration to Charles Darwin and anathema to Karl Marx. In the twentieth century, but especially since the 1960s, historians and demographers alike have come to regard *An Essay on the Principle of Population* as providing a model for the study of pre-industrial societies in western Europe and to see Malthus not only as one of the first economists, but also one of the great Georgian historians.

The model that characterises Malthus's principle, at least the one embodied in the second *Essay*, is best represented in diagramatic form. Figure 1 shows a systems model in which the rate of population growth is influenced by mortality, fertility and net migration (Wrigley, 1983a). The diagram should be read in the following way: if the rate of population growth begins to accelerate the price of food will be increased thus reducing the level of real wages; lower real wages may lead to increased mortality or adversely affect the prospects of marrying which will automatically increase the level of both temporary and permanent celibacy; fertility will accordingly be reduced and population growth decelerate as it would if mortality were to be increased. The narrow-lined arrows in Figure 1 are used to represent the positive check while the broader-lined arrows show the preventive check. The arrows made up of dashed lines are not strictly part of a Malthusian system while the arrows to mortality, real wages, food prices and marital fertility represent influences from outside the closed system marked by the rectangular outer box. Malthus's *Principle of Population* reduces very easily to a closed systems model dominated by negative feedback loops in which either mortality or fertility, influenced by nuptiality, provide routes by which population growth may be brought into balance with resources and prevailing economic conditions. The system is said to be 'homeostatic' or self-regulating and, if the mortality-positive check circuit dominates, to be a 'high-pressure system', but if the nuptiality/fertility-preventive check is more influential then to be a 'low-pressure system' (Wrigley and Schofield, 1981, *454–84*). The purpose of this distinction is to separate those societies in which misery and vice are

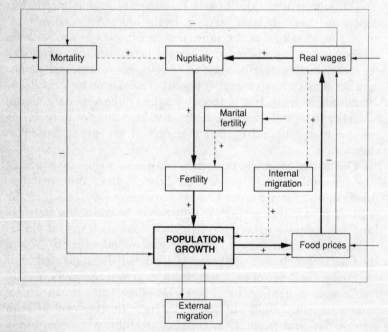

Figure 1 *A model of a demographic system*

endemic and those where moral restraint removes the need for a positive check. It is also logical to argue from Figure 1 that if fertility is effectively controlled via nuptiality, the rate of population growth is not only kept in harmony with prevailing resource supply, but the ratio of resources to population is actually improved, food prices should then fall and real wages increase. Thus there may be not only short-term economic advantages to be had from a well-adjusted preventive check, but for those societies having persistently high levels of celibacy, there may be long-term structural advantages for income per head and capital accumulation (Wrigley, 1988, *20–22*). As can be readily imagined, it has proved tempting to take the spirit of this argument further and to speculate that a contributory cause of early industrialization in Britain and north-west Europe was related to the comparative advantage conferred by the presence of a culturally embedded and thus rigidly adhered to form of the preventive check which condoned marriage only when financial means were sufficient for the establishment of a new and independent household by the newlyweds (Macfarlane, 1986 *35–48*; Anderson,1988a).

Figure 1 shows three other relationships which were not part of Malthus's original principle, but are nonetheless worthy of special comment. First, in agrarian societies one would expect the opportunity to marry to be associated with the supply of farms to be allocated via the rules for inheritance. If adult mortality were to increase for any reason it should serve to release more farms. In these particular circumstances it is possible to envisage real wages falling, mortality increasing and the opportunity to marry also increasing. Secondly, migration internal to the system will be stimulated by geographical inequalities in real wages. Thirdly, marital fertility, that is the birth of legitimate children to married women, will also contribute to the general level of fertility. In Malthus's scheme marital fertility is not linked with real wages and controls on it are not part of the preventive check. Fertility in marriage is not limited by deliberate human intervention; this would be an immoral act to be classed as vice.

The final reason for beginning with the *Principle of Population* and the systems model that so neatly summarises its salient features is that during the nineteenth century ways were found to escape from the weight of Malthus's law. What we have in Figure 1 provides a benchmark against which we may judge some of the most significant demographic changes to occur before the First World War. First, and of fundamental importance for the *Principle*, the association between population growth rates and food prices appears to have been broken during Malthus's lifetime (Wrigley and Schofield, 1981, *405*; Wrigley, 1983b, 1987, *215–41*, 1988, *63*).

Secondly, while the inverse association between mortality and real wages persisted, the latter began a long-run improvement. Mortality was probably reduced as a consequence, but differences between classes persisted and may even have been at their most accentuated towards the end of the nineteenth century. Improving standard of living was only one of many potential contributors to falling mortality.

Thirdly, marital fertility took the place of nuptiality as the principal influence on changes and variations in the general level of fertility. Family limitation came to be widely practised (Wilson and Woods, 1992).

Fourthly, the closed demographic system described by Malthus was thrown open to new forms of destabilising influences. Cities grew at the expense of villages; America and the Empire at the expense of Britain. The volume of internal migration rose rapidly; many thousands left for new worlds while others came to Britain seeking one.

Malthus could not have envisaged these changes. No one could in 1803, but his description of the race between the hare of population and the tortoise of subsistence is still of profound importance. His classification of the checks to population, but especially the stress he placed on the distinctive demographic role of marriage in western Europe, have only recently begun to be fully appreciated. He was probably unwise to lay so much emphasis on the inverse association between the preventive and the positive checks, since the two may work together, and to imply that economic as well as moral superiority could be conferred on those societies effectively using that form of the preventive check which stressed the age at which sexual activity commenced rather than when it stopped or how it was rationed.

2 What do we know and how do we know it?

Among the many epithets applied to the nineteenth century, the 'age of statistics' would seem one of the most appropriate. The first British population census was conducted in 1801 and repeated every ten years thereafter. The civil registration of births, deaths and marriages was begun in England and Wales in 1837 and 1855 in Scotland. While civil registration did not replace the recording of ecclesiastical events, particularly baptisms and burials, it did mean that parish registers lost their position as the principal source for demographic enquiry. In the second half of the nineteenth century information on the population's age structure, for example, drawn from the censuses, could be matched with data on age or cause of death from vital registration to create a relatively clear account at least of the pattern of mortality.

The availability of several guide books to sources of demographic and social statistics for the nineteenth century makes it unnecessary to dwell on the details of content, availability and accuracy (Wrigley, 1966, 1972; Lawton, 1978; Nissel, 1987; Higgs, 1989), but it may prove useful to provide some illustrations of how certain changes in content and reliability have affected the ability of contemporary and twentieth-century demographers to construct an accurate and comprehensive picture. As all historical demographers know only too well – sources condition interpretations.

First, the availability of a series of population censuses makes it a far more simple task to chart the changing size, composition – in terms of age and sex – and distribution of population. The problem Malthus had in his first *Essay* of knowing the true size of 'this Island's' population was thus removed by 1803 (Malthus, 1803, *14*). Table 1 gives totals for the population of England and Wales, Scotland and Ireland based on the 1801 to 1911 censuses, as well as those for 1931,

21

Table 1 *The Population of England and Wales, Scotland and
Ireland (in thousands)*

	England and Wales	Scotland	Ireland
Estimates			
1601	4,460		
1651	5,608		
1701	5,448	1,040	2,000
1751	6,222	1,265	2,250
1791			4,500
Censuses			
1801	8,893	1,608	
1811	10,164	1,806	
1821	12,000	2,092	6,802
1831	13,897	2,364	7,767
1841	15,914	2,620	8,178
1851	17,928	2,889	6,554
1861	20,066	3,062	5,799
1871	22,712	3,360	5,412
1881	25,974	3,736	5,175
1891	29,003	4,026	4,705
1901	32,528	4,472	4,459
1911	36,070	4,761	4,390
1931	39,952	4,843	
1951	43,758	5,096	4,332
1981	49,155	5,131	4,953
1991			

Percentage share of British Isles population	*1800*	*1900*
England	55	73
Wales	4	5
Scotland	10	11
Ireland	31	11

Source: based on Mitchell (1988)

1951 and 1981. It also shows estimates for dates prior to 1801. Great Britain's population was about 6.5 millions in 1701, 7.5 millions in 1751, 11 in 1801, 21 in 1851 and 37 in 1901, of which England's share increased from 77 per cent in the mid-eighteenth century to 82 per cent in 1901. Within this, London's share increased from 9 per cent to 12 per cent over the same period. By 1901 London's population was more than twice that of Wales and slightly more than that of Scotland. Although it is not a simple matter to define urban places, the 1850s is by convention taken as the decade in which half Britain's population can be classified as urban. The growth of London certainly made a substantial contribution to urbanization, but it was the expansion of provincial industrial and commercial centres, which created the great Victorian cities, that made a crucial difference to the national scene (Law, 1967; Lawton, 1972, 1983; Armstrong, 1981).

Secondly, the operation of a hundred years rule restricting the disclosure of information about individuals recorded in the nineteenth-century censuses has effectively limited public access to the more recent census enumerators' books. In the 1841 and subsequent censuses the enumerators were obliged to make copies of the household census schedules in specially printed ledgers. These books now provide invaluable information on named individuals, arranged by address and also relationship to head of household. Data on age, sex, marital status, occupation and place of birth are also provided (Lawton,1978). The ability to consider household structure, occupation, life-time migration, and to trace the characteristics of individuals and households from census to census has remarkably enhanced our knowledge of mid-Victorian society, but especially urban society.

Thirdly, the establishment of General Register Offices in London in 1837 and Edinburgh in 1855, the need for full-time specialist staffs well versed in statistical methods, and efficient nationwide administrations created a statistical bureaucracy with wide-ranging implications for both the collection and analysis of demographic data (Newsholme, 1889; Nissel, 1987). For example, the compilers of statistics at the London GRO were men of great distinction, all medically qualified, who brought a sense of rigour and purpose to what otherwise might have been merely a matter of data collection. The contribution of William Farr (1807–1883) must be singled out for special mention (Eyler, 1979). He was Compiler of Abstracts at the London GRO from 1839 to 1880, where for thirty-seven of those years he worked closely with George Graham, the Registrar General. Farr was responsible for calculating the first official English life tables, preparing special reports on cholera, devising classifications of cause of death and innumerable other small yet, in combination, significant improvements in the system of recording, its detail and accuracy (Farr, 1864, 1885).

In England and Wales the registration system was organized in the following way. The country was divided into registration divisions, counties and districts, many of the most populous of which were further divided into sub-districts. Each registration district had a Superintendent Registrar whose responsibility it was to gather the required information on births, deaths and marriages and forward it to London where it would be compiled, tabulated and to some extent interpreted in the *Annual Reports* and *Decennial Supplements*. The sub-districts, districts (over 600 by 1851) and counties (45) provided the units for reporting, but convention varied with GRO interest and administrative convenience.

Farr himself was probably responsible for the emphasis on mortality statistics which were derived from death certificates. Since the age, sex, occupation and cause of death of the deceased were all recorded on these certificates, fairly detailed tables giving numbers dying classified by age, sex, occupation, cause and place of death could be created. Compared with the tables may be derived from the birth certificates, these are truly rich veins to be mined. Fertility was not a subject of great public concern in Victorian Britain, although it became so in the early 1900s. The number of births, their sex and legitimacy was reported, but not the age of the mother or further details about her previous pregnancies, the duration of her marriage, her and her husband's occupations etc. In Scotland in 1855 the practice of recording maternal age was begun, but it was discontinued in 1856. The effects of these major lacunae on our ability to reconstruct nineteenth-century fertility patterns will be obvious. Crude and indirectly standardized rates may be calculated, but little more. Marriage was of rather more concern to Victorians, largely because of its standing in law, but here too there are limitations. From the marriage certificates, the GRO regularly tabulated the number of marriages, the form of solemnization (civil or ecclesiastical and thence denomination) and whether the bride and groom were able to put their own signatures to the certificate. Estimates of literacy levels have been based on the last-mentioned piece of information (see Figure 6 for example). Despite these various problems, the development of civil registration from 1837 or 1855, coupled with considerable improvements in the population censuses from 1841, means that it is the demography of the first third or half of the nineteenth century that remains obscure in comparison with later decades.

Having outlined the origins and development of population data gathering in the nineteenth century, we are now able to return to the question: what do we know about the changing demography of Britain?

Population, its composition and distribution

We have already seen in Table 1 that the population of Britain increased substantially in the nineteenth century, but it also changed in composition and distribution. While it is no simple matter to trace the changing employment, occupation and social class structure of Britain between 1801 and 1911 via the census, a start may be made for certain distinctive groups of occupations and considerable detail is possible for the last fifty years. Of the major categories of employment, agriculture was in steep relative decline at mid-century, representing only about 20 per cent of those employed; manufacturing was holding steady at about 33 per cent; domestic service contributed 14 to 15 per cent and the remaining 32 per cent was made up from mining, building, transport, dealing, and the professions and public service in roughly equal measure. By the end of the century agriculture's contribution to employment was no more than 10 per cent. These figures do, of course, conceal major differences in the sexual division of

Table 2 *The Social Class Composition of England and Wales*

Social class	1881	(%)	1911	(%)	Change index
1951 classification					
I	159,756	(2)	302,753	(3)	126
II	1,089,498	(15)	1,729,865	(15)	105
III	2,972,127	(40)	4,863,747	(43)	108
IV	2,276,383	(30)	3,303,648	(29)	96
V	974,034	(13)	1,101,402	(10)	75
1911 classification					
VI	361,928		428,658		78
VII	407,532		881,716		142
VIII	740,554		595,600		53
Example occupations					
Doctors	15,091		24,553		107
Civil servants	19,556		61,152		206
Commercial clerks	173,161		353,622		134
Farmers	203,308		208,750		68
Grocers	99,434		161,528		107
Railway employees	194,541		425,588		144
Carpenters, joiners	226,214		207,253		60
Tailors	98,919		120,494		80
Tramway service	2,591		41,219		1,047
Electricity supply	2,447		98,089		2,637

The 1951 classification
I - professional and managerial occupations
II - intermediate non-manual
III - skilled manual
IV - intermediate manual
V - unskilled manual
The 1911 classification used three special groups
VI - textile workers
VII - miners
VIII - agricultural workers
Change index: [(1911/1881)/k] x 100, where k is the ratio of total classified in 1911 to 1881 (ie 1.52).
Source: based on Banks (1978)

labour. Domestic servants were overwhelmingly young women while agricultural labourers were generally male; agricultural servants and female gangs of the eastern counties of England and Scotland, used especially in harvesting vegetables and root crops, were the major exceptions. Those engaged in manufacturing were also predominantly male, female textile workers represent the principal exception. Most women employees, at least those recorded in the census, were not married (Hewitt, 1958; Roberts, 1984).

The information on occupations in the 1851 and 1911 censuses is sufficiently detailed to encourage those interested in defining broad social classes; yet all those tempted to engage in social grading have faced considerable problems in making their classifications (Szreter, 1984). Table 2 provides evidence for the continued rise of the middle class, the growth

Table 3 *Population Redistribution and Urbanization in England and Wales (figures are given in parts per thousand)*

| | Rural | In towns of: | | | | Urban |
		2,500–10,000	10,000–50,000	50,000–100,000	Over 100,000	
1801	662	99	94	35	110	338
1811	634	108	94	37	137	366
1821	600	109	92	43	156	400
1831	557	106	111	40	186	443
1841	527	100	121	55	207	483
1851	460	99	135	58	248	540
1861	413	98	140	61	288	587
1871	348	108	162	56	326	652
1881	300	105	160	73	362	700
1891	255	102	163	86	394	745
1901	220	89	181	74	436	780
1911	211	88	183	80	438	789

Urban plus Rural equals 1,000 and the sum of the four town size categories equals Urban.
Source: based on Law (1967)

of bureaucracy and transport services; the further decline of agricultural employment; the decline of certain skilled trades dominated by the self-employed; and the dramatic expansion of the new energy industries. However, Table 2 does not provide evidence for radical change in the class structure, merely a shift of the unskilled into other occupations, many of which required more skill and certainly more specialization. At least 75 per cent of late Victorian Britain's population was made up of the urban industrial working class and their children (Booth, 1886; Banks, 1978; Routh, 1987).

Table 3 shows the changing distribution of population between urban and rural places, large and small towns. It complements the points illustrated in Table 2. By 1911 Britain was overwhelmingly an urban country in which large commercial and industrial cities predominated. None could compete with London, yet each held sway in its own region (Weber, 1889; Lawton, 1958, 1983).

Demographic change

Apart from the rise of great cities the nineteenth century was also a period of significant if not dramatic demographic change. Mortality began its secular decline, to be reinforced at the turn of the century by the rapid decline of infant mortality. General fertility rates were in decline throughout the century, but from the 1870s marital fertility also began its secular decline. The causes of these revolutionary changes are still not understood with any degree of certainty, as we shall see in later chapters; nor can their trends and characteristics be charted with the precision and confidence one would wish (Glass, 1951; Teitelbaum, 1974). Table 4 makes a start. It gives estimated series for the crude birth and death rates (CBR, CDR), life expectation at birth (e_0), infant mortality (IMR), the gross reproduction rate (GRR) and the index of overall fertility (I_f). All of the measures reported in Table 4, but especially those for periods 1 to 12, need to be treated with extreme caution; they are merely guides to approximate orders of magnitude.

Despite these reservations Table 4, accompanied by Figure 2 which shows long-run fertility and mortality trends

Table 4 *Demographic Indices for England, 1551–1850, and England and Wales, 1851–1975*

Twenty-five year periods	CBR	CDR	e_0	IMR	GRR	I_f
1 1551–75	34.94	28.42	35	190	2.41	0.345
2 1576–1600	33.22	24.22	39	162	2.29	0.336
3 1601–25	32.72	24.82	39	162	2.25	0.324
4 1626–50	31.46	26.22	36	178	2.11	0.310
5 1651–75	28.58	28.36	35	189	1.91	0.271
6 1676–1700	31.22	30.28	33	199	2.07	0.311
7 1701–25	31.74	27.86	36	180	2.23	0.327
8 1726–50	33.74	30.50	33	203	2.25	0.335
9 1751–75	34.24	27.26	36	180	2.38	0.348
10 1776–1800	35.56	26.46	37	175	2.64	0.389
11 1801–25	40.18	25.38	39	167	2.91	0.423
12 1826–50	36.04	22.54	40	151	2.57	0.365
13 1851–75	35.82	22.22	41	154	2.49	0.360
14 1876–1900	32.28	19.26	46	149	2.07	0.313
15 1901–25	24.02	14.26	53	105	1.42	0.233
16 1926–50	16.16	12.24	64	55	0.95	0.174
17 1951–75	16.76	11.72	72	22	1.15	0.188

CBR - crude birth rate
CDR - crude death rate
e_0 - life expectancy at birth in years
IMR - infant mortality rate
GRR - gross reproduction rate
I_f - index of overall fertility
See the *Glossary of Demographic Terms* for definitions
Sources: based on Wrigley and Schofield (1981) and Wilson and Woods (1992)

(measured by GRR and e_0), helps us to place the nineteenth century in context. It was a period of transition from an old demographic regime characterized by the form of system illustrated in Figure 1 and associated with Malthus, to a new regime in which mortality is now very low, almost all deaths occur in old age and average life expectation at birth is approaching its maximum at about 90 to 92 years. Contraceptives are available, effective and used to achieve small completed family sizes and to time conceptions in order to maximise female employment opportunities. Marriage is less necessary and divorce is common. Several of these radical changes began and became obvious before the First World War; others have only emerged in the last three decades (Anderson, 1985, 1990).

It is also worth emphasising at this point that some of the most important changes in demographic structure were not particular to Britain alone. Figure 3 shows the influence of changes in fertility and mortality on the intrinsic rate of natural population increase (r) for England, France and Sweden between 1751 and 1981. The diagonal lines join points with equal rates of natural increase, allowing the relative contributions of fertility and mortality to be judged more easily (Wrigley and Schofield, 1981, *246*). In each case fertility and mortality have declined since the late eighteenth century, but the time paths for the three countries so traced vary quite

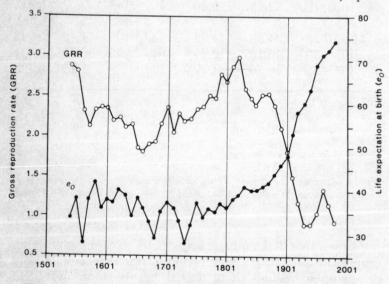

Figure 2 *Long-term trends in English fertility (gross reproduction rate) and mortality (life expectation at birth).*

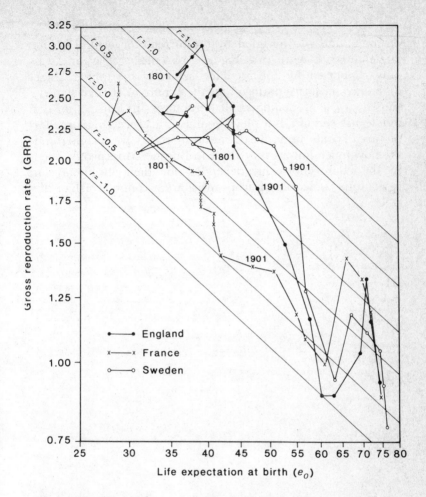

Figure 3 *The influence of changes in fertility (gross reproduction rate) and mortality (life expectation at birth) on the intrinsic rate of natural population increase (r) for England, France and Sweden, 1751 to 1981.*

markedly. In France fertility and mortality declined together from an early date and natural growth remained at a low level throughout the nineteenth century. In Sweden mortality declined before fertility in a way that has come to be regarded as normal and coincidental with the predictions of the classic demographic transition model. But in England the modern rise

31

of population was initiated by the increase of fertility in the late eighteenth century, as Figure 2 also makes clear, and was only supported by the secular decline of mortality. These differences of form, pattern and the timing of change suggest the diversity of demographic structures in Europe in the nineteenth century, but they also illustrate aspects of a broader picture of conformity. Fertility and mortality were higher and are now much lower everywhere in Europe. Most people lived in the countryside and depended for their livelihood on agriculture, now most Europeans share a common urban life style.

3   Whether to move and where to go

In any consideration of nineteenth-century population history
pride of place should go to mobility and migration, both
internal and international. Not only did Britain's population
experience radical redistribution, but the age-, sex- and skill-
selective nature of migration also changed society, economy
and environment in several very important respects, some of
which will be considered separately in Chapters 4 and 6.

Four aspects are of particular significance. First, the outer
rural periphery – especially the west of Ireland and the
Scottish Highlands – experienced massive emigration which
caused general depopulation (Flinn, 1977; Anderson and
Morse, 1990; Withers and Watson 1991). Although the Irish
case is often linked to famine migration in the 1840s, the
history of Irish emigration to North America and Great Britain
is a long one which famine probably only exacerbated (see
Table 1). Secondly, the countryside in general suffered net loss
to the towns (Saville, 1957; Lawton,1967). From Cornwall to
Norfolk, Dorset to Anglesey and Aberdeen agricultural
labourers, servants and small tenants left and were not
replaced, except by machines. In a few rural counties, such
as Kent, this did not lead to absolute population decline
because natural growth exceeded net out-migration, but in
most counties the downward spiral of decline was not arrested
until after the Second World War (Lawton, 1968). Thirdly,
the great industrial and commercial centres of central
Scotland, the English North and Midlands, and South
Wales, not only increased their citizenry, but also expanded
physically until they coalesced into the amorphous
conurbations so well known in the twentieth century. These
Victorian cities grew particularly rapidly both by net
migration and natural growth, despite high mortality. Intra-
urban migration also fuelled suburban expansion which

eventually affected whole cities, primarily through the depopulation of their inner areas. In the cases of certain Scottish and Northern industrial towns this process was obvious even in the late nineteenth century (Lawton, 1983; Morris, 1990). Fourthly, London should probably be treated as a special case since it not only maintained its British primacy, but also its share of the total population. The new problems associated with managing and servicing such a massive concentration of people – nearly five millions by 1901 – imposed many strains, not least in terms of transport, social inequalities which were made more obvious by their juxtaposition, and sanitation. The engineering problems were solved in time; the others still remain.

Of course this is a very simple view of migration which, while acceptable in outline, is thwarted by paucity of sources and complexity of process when more detail is required. In the 1991 census, migration was recorded by asking respondents where they were living one year ago, but for Victorian Britain place of birth must suffice. International migration must be counted by using embarkation lists. Although the general flow of migrants has turned from rural-urban to urban-urban to urban-rural over the last two hundred years, the pattern of any one individual's moves through his or her lifetime might include many addresses and several towns or villages. Step, chain and return migration are all appropriate terms, as is circulatory movement. However, migration need not be regarded as a series of random walks; there is order in the chaos once one deals with aggregates.

Emigration

The broad picture of European migration shows that from 1821 to 1915 44 millions left, of which Great Britain accounted for 10 and Ireland for 6 millions. More detailed estimates suggest that between 1853 and 1900 4,675,100 persons left England and Wales for a non-European destination while 896,000 left Scotland. In both cases more than half went to the USA with a further fifth to Australasia (Carrier and Jeffrey, 1953; Easterlin, 1961; Baines, 1985).

Although these figures are impressive in their own right, the

34

impact of emigration needs to be assessed with some caution. For example, if the annual rate of emigration per thousand population for England and Wales in the second half of the nineteenth century was to be set at 1, then the corresponding figures for Scotland and Ireland would be 1.4 and 3.1, with 2 and 4 in several decades. Emigration was far more important for Irish and Scottish populations than it was for England. Between 1853 and 1900 net emigration represented 9 per cent of natural increase in England and Wales, but more than 25 per cent for Scotland. It is also important to note that of the 4,675,100 who left England and Wales between 1853 and 1900 only about 2,250,000 were permanent migrants, giving England and Wales what was probably an unusually high rate of return migration compared with Scotland, Ireland and the rest of Europe (Baines, 1985).

To continue our catalogue of complications, let us briefly consider the Irish in Britain. In 1851, 7.2 per cent of the population of Scotland and 2.9 per cent of the population of England and Wales had been born in Ireland. The other nineteenth-century censuses give averages of 5.5 and 2.0 per cent, respectively, for Scotland and England and Wales (Lawton, 1959). Within Great Britain the towns of the west of Scotland, the north west and Midlands of England and London were particularly popular temporary or permanent destinations. But cities like Liverpool and Glasgow were also important ports for re-embarkation to America, thus allowing Irish-born migrants to become emigrants from England or Scotland (Lawton, 1956; Lees, 1979; Swift and Gilley, 1985).

Urbanization

Although it is now useful to consider inter-regional migration in its own right, in nineteenth-century Britain movement was more specifically to the cities, coastal resorts and the coalfields. Any region possessing one or a number of these was likely to receive migrants from its neighbours. It is therefore appropriate to consider internal migration in terms of selective urban growth and rural decline (Redford, 1926; Cairncross, 1953; Friedlander and Roshier, 1966).

Even in 1801 England was highly urbanized, with about 30

per cent of its population living in urban places and perhaps another 36 per cent living in rural areas but not directly engaged in agriculture. (The rural agricultural population of France was still nearly 60 per cent of the total at this time.) The 'half urban' mark had been crossed by 1851 in England and Wales, slightly later in Scotland, and by the early years of the twentieth century at least three-quarters of the population were urban residents. Most migrants came from the same or neighbouring counties. The rural surplus population of the countryside was often replaced if not actually displaced by new labour-saving technology, or else attracted by expanding industries offering higher wages to work in the factories or mines. Many migrants, the more skilled in particular, changed place of employment and residence without changing the nature of their jobs. Coal to coal, iron to iron, port to port, kitchen to kitchen, loom to loom: this was an important element in the process of internal redistribution and economic development. Labour was as mobile and as adept as capital at seeking out and responding to relative advantage.

However, it must be emphasised that although migration was an important contributor to urbanization, most nineteenth-century towns and cities also grew by natural increase. This was itself a reflection of biases in the age- and sex-selective nature of rural to urban migration which tended to pick out the young and active, and to leave behind the elderly or less ambitious. In England and Wales, the total population living in urban registration districts increased by some 182 per cent between 1841 and 1911, of which 151 per cent was due to natural increase and 31 per cent to net migration. In rural registration districts there was a 13 per cent overall gain in population made up of 86 per cent natural increase and 73 per cent net migration loss (Lawton, 1967, 1968, 1980, 1983). Of the non-rural districts, the very large cities, the resorts and residential centres, and the coalfield settlements grew most rapidly because natural growth was supplemented by migration gain; this was not only at the expense of rural areas, but of the smaller and middle-sized towns, many of which failed to expand by net migration and some of which were net exporters of people. By the end of the nineteenth century the rural share of Britain's population had begun to stabilize; migration had changed to become largely inter-urban or intra-urban and directed towards the upper-end of the urban settlement hierarchy, or to be distinctly residential and short distance in character, reflecting changes of residence but not necessarily places of employment (Lawton, 1979; Pooley, 1979; Dennis, 1984). While the purely demographic impact of migration declined, the social and environmental legacy remained. Places created and filled in the nineteenth century have been rejected and depleted in the twentieth.

'Laws' and causes

Although we shall never know the particular form of motivations that led individuals to migrate, it is reasonable to infer some of the principal causes from the most obvious patterns of mass movement. When E. G. Ravenstein (1834–1913) defined his 'laws of migration' in the 1870s and 1880s he saw the major causes of migration as economic in nature, leading young adults from the great centres of industry and commerce (Ravenstein, 1885, 1889). In general there seems little reason to doubt this conclusion, but points for debate remain over whether the migrants were pushed or pulled, the extent to which entire families were involved, the balance between males and females, the stepped nature of the movement, and the extent to which localized changes of address outweighed, in volume if not in significance, the longer-distance rural-urban migration with which Ravenstein was so concerned (Grigg, 1977).

It is clear from both historical studies and recent surveys that the volume of migration will increase when both push and pull factors are working, but also when origins and potential destinations are well connected by both easy access and a ready flow of information. If there is no transport, only the brave or the very desperate will pioneer the route; no information and the move depends on serendipity; no push and inertia will hold sway; no pull and alternative destinations may prove more attractive. The late nineteenth-century Atlantic economy seems to have provided all the necessary conditions (Thomas, 1954; Baines, 1985). The British and

American economic cycles were out of phase, British slump coincided with American boom; steamships made the passage cheaper and somewhat more comfortable; friends and relatives established in the USA and Canada provided information and assistance.

The same observation could also be made regarding internal migration in the British Isles. The longer-distance pioneer migrants were largely motivated by employment prospects, whether that meant rural-urban movement in the early decades of the nineteenth century or urban-urban in later years. The spread of the railway network was a great boon, but the bicycle also played its part by enhancing local mobility (Perry, 1969). Relatives and friends followed the pioneers and those simply looking for a better place to live, without necessarily changing jobs, made up the numbers.

4 Marriage

We know from earlier chapters that the preventive check and moral restraint played an important part in Britain's demography. The marriage pattern of north-western Europe was rather distinctive, not to say eccentric, in comparison with other southern or eastern European, or non-European societies. Marriage was not universal and it did not take place very quickly after menarche. Generally, it was not arranged by parents, but was a matter of free choice between eligible partners heavily constrained by social and geographical barriers. Marriage usually, at least for women, coincided with the start of sexual activity, and led to the establishment of a new household distinct from both sets of parents. While marriage may have required their approval, it also signalled independence from parental control and responsibility. However, this may prove to be a rather idealised picture. A substantial minority of brides were pregnant. Many young people had already left their parental home and its influence long before getting married. Others retained close social contacts in the same community even after forming a separate household (Anderson, 1980; Wall, Robin and Laslett, 1983).

This chapter is primarily concerned with the timing of marriage and the extent of nuptiality, their temporal and geographical variations and their influence on fertility. The next chapter deals with the limitation of fertility within marriage and the more intimate relations between husbands and wives.

What should our expectations be with respect to Georgian and Victorian marriage patterns? Many of our perceptions have been encouraged by Jane Austen and her characterization of the Bennet family of Longbourn, Hertfordshire, and others in similar social positions. During 24 years of marriage Mr and Mrs Bennet had been blessed with five daughters. The youngest, a well-grown girl of 16, eloped with a soldier who was only obliged to marry her after the negotiation of a financial settlement. The eldest, a sweet girl of 23 who smiled too much, made a good match with a young man from the North of England, the recent inheritor of industrial wealth. The second at 21 made a brilliant match with a man of great substance, much of it located in Derbyshire. The marital fortunes of the other daughters remain obscure, but it is to be supposed that the third, a plain girl, remained a spinster at home reading, adjusting her ideas and caring for her parents. Now, of course, one must not be tempted to think the Bennets typical of their age, but their fears and prejudices probably reflect closely a preoccupation with the need for a woman to marry carefully, if not well.

> Without thinking highly either of men or matrimony, marriage had always been her object; it was the only honourable provision for well-educated young women of small fortune, and however uncertain of giving happiness, must be their pleasantest preservative from want. This preservative she had now obtained; and at the age of twenty-seven, without having ever been handsome, she felt all the good luck of it.

Thus the thoughts of a friend of the Misses Bennet on accepting the proposal of a cleric whom she regarded as neither sensible nor agreeable, and whose society was irksome to her.

In wider society the prospects for marriage were affected by the size of the pool of eligibles, its composition and the circumstances in which those eligibles found themselves. To complicate matters, we must also remember that many young women left home in their late teens to become domestic or farm servants (Higgs, 1983; Anderson, 1984; Hinde, 1985; Litchfield, 1988); that in certain areas of the country most women spent some time employed in the textile industry (Hewitt, 1958); that a significant group of young women were obliged to marry because they had become pregnant; that widows and widowers often remarried; and that just because divorce was restricted we should not think separation uncommon (Stone, 1990).

In broad terms, the level of nuptiality declined throughout the nineteenth and early twentieth century in England and Wales, but it did so from the high peak of the late Georgian years (Wilson and Woods, 1992). After the 1850s in both England and Wales and Scotland the rate of change was relatively slow until the increase of the late 1930s and 1940s. Increasingly, marriage was postponed until the mid- to late-twenties and many did not marry at all. In itself this is an interesting, if imprecise, observation yet it is the geography of Victorian marriage patterns that holds the key to our understanding of nuptiality's variable demographic contribution, at least in the late nineteenth century, rather than its slow change over time (Woods, 1992). Regional, but especially local, variations would appear to reflect some of the influences outlined above. If this does prove to be the case, then a consideration of the geography of nuptiality will not only assist our appreciation of how fertility declined in late Victorian Britain, but it will also provide a simple summary of the effects of age- and sex-selective migration; occupational specialization; employment opportunities; the distribution of eligible partners; and local customs.

The geography of nuptiality

Using index I_m, the proportion of females married, Table 5 shows the extent of nuptiality in the late nineteenth century. It quotes I_m for England and Wales, Scotland and selected registration counties. Its purpose is to illustrate slow change over the fifty years as well as the extent of regional diversity. As is often the case, extremes are of most interest. The highest levels of nuptiality were to be found among those populations living in coalmining communities where there was usually a surplus of eligible men whose wages peaked early in their working lives and where alternative employment for women was scarce (Friedlander, 1973). West Lothian and Durham provide good examples. At the other extreme we have rural populations which had been exposed to very substantial emigration and in which there were few economic opportunities either in or outside agriculture. Sutherland, in the north of Scotland, was the most striking example. The other examples drawn from rural Scotland, Wigtownshire and Aberdeenshire, show higher levels of nuptiality, but in the former the level was increasing while in the latter it was in decline (Anderson and Morse, 1990). In the English rural counties of Norfolk and Wiltshire there was very slow decline.

Table 5 *Index of Proportion Married, I_m*

	1861	1891	1911
England and Wales	0.502	0.477	0.479
London	0.483	0.459	0.444
Lancashire	0.504	0.482	0.478
County Durham	0.593	0.564	0.552
Norfolk	0.498	0.492	0.469
Wiltshire	0.499	0.487	0.488
Scotland	0.422	0.420	0.418
Sutherland	0.295	0.322	0.319
Aberdeenshire	0.393	0.383	0.325
Wigtownshire	0.370	0.373	0.380
Midlothian	0.394	0.397	0.391
West Lothian	0.569	0.563	0.573
Ireland		0.336	0.339

See the *Glossary of Demographic Terms* for definitions.
Source: based on Coale and Watkins (1986).

While the index I_m does capture the general volume of marriage, it also obscures the individual effects of age at marriage and the proportion ultimately marrying. For, while one would expect late marriage and low proportions marrying to be related, the association need not be a perfect one. While we cannot be absolutely certain, it seems most likely that the geographical variation in nuptiality, conveniently captured by I_m, was due mainly to differences in the proportion of women who remained unmarried during their thirties and forties rather than to differences in the proportion of women who had married by the age of twenty-five. While the mean age at marriage might vary very little, those left unmarried at thirty could account for from 5 to 30 per cent or more of women (Anderson, 1984).

The importance of these distinctions may be clarified by imagining particular forms of economy and society. Consider the differences between Sutherland or western Ireland, a textile town like Keighley in the West Riding of Yorkshire, and a city such as Bath with many wealthy residents and visitors employing substantial numbers of domestic servants. In Sutherland the opportunity to marry would be limited for financial reasons even if the sex ratio of eligibles was balanced. Many holdings were not sufficiently large to support a wife and children. In Keighley young women would usually spend some time, perhaps ten years working in the mills before they married (Garrett, 1990). The mean age at first marriage might be increased, but not necessarily the ultimate proportion getting married. And in Bath, where female domestic servants were numerous, being 'in service' would have represented a 'stage in the life cycle' prior to marriage and starting a family as well as a source of refuge for the widowed or abandoned. Here Sutherland, Keighley and Bath stand proxy for other equivalent areas in the rest of Britain.

Among London's registration districts there was a very close inverse relationship between I_m and the percentage of women employed in domestic service. In Hampstead I_m was 0.274 while in Poplar, in the East End, it was 0.638 in 1861 and little changed in 1891 (Woods, 1984). Indeed, the range of I_m values between London registration districts was greater than among registration counties in the British Isles.

So far in this chapter we have taken note of certain social conventions in marriage, at least as portrayed in literature, considered variations in the extent of nuptiality, particularly its geographical manifestation, and noted the contribution certain forms of labour organization can have for both age- and sex-selective migration and for the prospects of marrying. But since this pamphlet is largely concerned with demographic issues, we must now turn to consider the influence of nuptiality on fertility. In Britain in the early 1990s up to a third of babies were born outside marriage and about a third of marriages ended in divorce. In the last century marriage set the bounds for sexual activity; of course that does not mean that illegitimacy, bridal pregnancy, prostitution and adultery were not common especially in certain localities, but it does

Table 6 *Index of Illegitimate Fertility,* I_h

	1861	1891	1911
England and Wales	0.046	0.026	0.019
London	0.025	0.018	0.016
Lancashire	0.048	0.025	0.017
County Durham	0.062	0.035	0.027
Norfolk	0.074	0.043	0.030
Wiltshire	0.051	0.027	0.020
Scotland	0.056	0.042	0.031
Sutherland	0.022	0.024	0.020
Aberdeenshire	0.089	0.069	0.056
Wigtownshire	0.074	0.076	0.057
Midlothian	0.047	0.034	0.024
West Lothian	0.084	0.072	0.041
Ireland		0.010	0.010

See Table 5

give nuptiality a direct demographic significance which it has all but lost by now.

Table 6 illustrates the point using another fertility index I_h, illegitimate or non-marital fertility. If we begin by taking these figures at their face value and do not consider their level simply a reflection of attitudes to bastardy (where it is frowned upon, registration may be avoided) then they should suggest some interesting observations regarding the potential contribution of nuptiality to fertility rates. In post-famine Ireland virtually all births were to married women, but in north-east and south-west Scotland, East Anglia and eastern England in general, the extent of illegitimacy in 1861 was sufficiently large for one to begin to doubt the importance of marriage as a social and legal event with a strong demographic significance (16 per cent of births were illegitimate in Aberdeenshire) (Leneman and Mitchison, 1987; Mitchison and Leneman, 1989). But elsewhere in Britain, and especially off the coalfields, non-marital fertility was low enough at mid-century (only 5 or 6 per cent of births were illegitimate) for the institution of marriage still to be accepted as having particular significance as a regulator of fertility rates. But Table 6 also shows that by the early twentieth century I_h had fallen everywhere (only 4 per cent of births were illegitimate in England and Wales in 1911). Were those forces which initiated the decline of marital fertility also leading to the reduction of non-marital fertility?

5 How many children should we have?

The origins of the secular decline of marital fertility in Britain, as in much of western Europe with the exception of France, are to be found in the second half, but especially the last quarter of the nineteenth century. This much at least is clear from the available vital statistics, but there are many aspects of this fundamental change in demographic structure that remain obscure. By what means was the size of families limited? Why did marital fertility decline from this period and not earlier or later? Were the reasons economic or social in origin, of necessity or through the choice of fashion? Who controlled their fertility first and did others learn from their behaviour? Hypotheses abound, but the evidence remains tantalising in its vagueness or insecurity.

We do know that until the 1870s English, and by implication British, marital fertility was consistent with 'natural fertility', that is it was largely biologically determined with little sign of parity-specific control. Children came by God's will. In general, their births were neither deliberately spaced nor were there attempts to prevent conception or live birth once a particular number of children had already been born. A woman's fertility was influenced by her physiological ability to conceive, her proneness to spontaneous abortion, and the frequency of coitus. The first mentioned declined with age, the second increased, while the last mentioned declined with the duration of marriage (Bongaarts and Potter, 1983; Wilson, 1984, 1986).

Figure 4 shows age-specific marital fertility schedules for rural England, marriage cohorts 1550 to 1849 (Wilson and Woods, 1992); Scotland in 1855 (Hinde and Woods, 1984); the Hutterite marriage cohorts of 1921–30 (Coale and Watkins, 1986); and for comparison England and Wales in 1981. The height of each curve gives the level of total marital

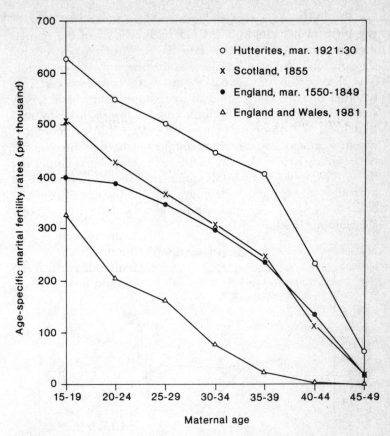

Figure 4 *Age-specific marital fertility curves.*

fertility, while the shape indicates whether any form of parity-specific control, or stopping behaviour, is present. The concave form of the modern England and Wales curve shows that effective family limitation is widespread, especially among married women in their thirties and forties. The convexity of the other three indicates that such stopping behaviour was either absent or unusual. Between the 1850s and the 1930s such behaviour became widespread in Britain; the level of age-specific marital fertility was much reduced and the shape of the resulting curve radically altered. Unfortunately, it is not possible to chart the exact course of the changing pattern of marital fertility because the recording of the mother's age at the birth of her children did not become part of the regular registration system until the late 1930s. The first year of civil registration in Scotland, 1855, was the one and only exception. Thus, it is also impossible to say with complete certainty whether married couples began by fixing on some ideal family size and then attempted to limit conceptions in order to meet that ideal (i.e. stopping behaviour – 'four and no more') or whether, at least initially, they sought to lengthen the intervals between births and thereby to affect the completed family size by, for example, consciously practising sexual abstinence in marriage (i.e. spacing behaviour). In the absence of contrary evidence, stopping behaviour is assumed more likely (Seccombe, 1990).

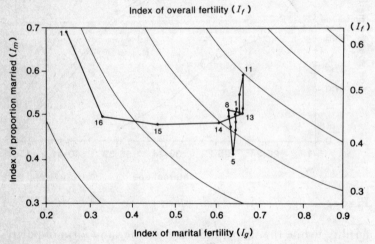

Figure 5 *The changing contribution of nuptiality (I_m) and marital fertility (I_g) to overall fertility (I_f) in England. (Each point represents a twenty-five year period as in Table 4. Point 1 is for 1551–75, 11 for 1801–25, 14 for 1876–1900 and 17 for 1951–75.) Source: Wilson and Woods (1992)*

Despite the paucity of data in a form that would be ideal for our purposes, it is nonetheless possible to be clear on the following points. First, unlike the increase in fertility in the late eighteenth and early nineteenth century, the experience of the late Victorian period was dominated by the secular decline of marital fertility and not a cyclical, perhaps isolated, movement in nuptiality (Woods, 1987; Wilson and Woods, 1992; see also Figures 2 and 3). Figure 5 plots I_m against I_g to reveal the highly distinctive nature of new trends originating in the third quarter of the nineteenth century (point 13 for 1851–75) when I_m (nuptiality) gave way to I_g (marital fertility) as the driving force of temporal changes in the level of fertility. Secondly, we may now assume in a way that was not open to contemporaries that marital fertility was reduced as the direct consequence of changed behaviour rather than some general decline in fecundity. Patterns of thought and action changed rather than physiology (Teitelbaum, 1984). Thirdly, and here we are on less sure ground, it is unlikely that the phenomenon was merely a result of the invention, marketing, adoption and effective use of new appliance methods of birth control. The rubber condom, Dutch cap and douche all became available during the last decades of the nineteenth century, but they were rather expensive for general use until the 1920s and 1930s when even the results of retrospective surveys reveal their far more widespread adoption (Peel, 1963). Since it is known that marital fertility was significantly reduced, it must be assumed that some combination of sexual abstinence, *coitus interruptus*, accurate use of the safe period (not properly understood until the twentieth century) and induced abortion were the most likely means by which family limitation was brought about. None of these methods was new to Victorians, but the desire and confidence to use them were innovatory (Shorter, 1973; McLaren, 1978; Sauer, 1978; Soloway, 1982).

If the foregoing represents sound, if unsubstantiated, reasoning, then how should we proceed to explain the obvious demographic trends? Let us, for the sake of clarity, over-simplify and consider only three possible approaches: the demographic, the economic and the sociological.

There is a persistent line of argument in demographic theory which holds that high levels of fertility are necessary to match high levels of mortality, and thus that when infant or childhood mortality begin to decline, marital fertility will also be reduced without adversely affecting the effective level of fertility, that is the supply of new adults capable of reproducing (Brass and Kabir, 1980; Teitelbaum, 1984; Woods, 1987). Thus mortality

49

decline not only facilitates the reduction of fertility, it also acts as a strong inducement. Setting aside for the time being any consideration of what causes mortality patterns to vary, it is still obvious that for this particular demographic mechanism to work there must be a distinct time lag between the decline of mortality and fertility during which average family size will increase. Married couples would be impelled to limit their fertility thereby avoiding the accompanying financial burdens which the survival of larger numbers of children would bring. This interpretation assumes that there is a distinct chronology to demographic change and that a sophisticated adjustment mechanism is created requiring considerable foresight on the part of married couples and a degree of reproductive planning. In Britain, childhood mortality certainly did decline at the same time as marital fertility, but infant mortality did not begin its secular decline until 1899–1900 (Woods, Watterson and Woodward, 1988). It seems likely that the reduction of infant and childhood mortality did eventually help to sustain marital fertility decline, but that mortality decline was not an initiating factor (Reves, 1985; Coale and Watkins,1986, *201–33*).

Economists have provided one of the most important theoretical contributions to the study of fertility. Their focus has tended to emphasise the costs and returns of having children, the costs and availability of contraceptive methods, inter-generational wealth flows, and the conflict between investing in children or consumer durables. Children, especially in traditional peasant societies, represent a source of labour, income and security for their parents. But in nineteenth-century urban Britain the economic value of children to their parents was far less obvious and presumably far less likely to enter any accounting framework for reproductive planning. In general, if parents were not attempting to maximize their fertility in order to reap financial gains for the family wage economy, they were also not attempting, until after the 1870s, to restrict their fertility in order to avoid the liability of childrearing (Haines, 1979; Crafts,1984a, 1984b). Remember also that it was rather unusual at this time and in most areas for married women to be employed outside the home, for reasons of tradition and lack of opportunity, and thus that childbearing and rearing

50

did not represent alternatives to wage earning as they do today. The sexual division of labour was clear; while he earned, she looked after him, home and children.

Set against this rather confusing picture we have the concepts of 'relative income compression' and 'social diffusion'. During the late nineteenth century, it is claimed, middle class parents were obliged to devote increasing proportions of their incomes to the education of their children in order to provide them with competitive advantage in the labour market (Banks, 1954). They were also tempted to alter their spending patterns towards status-conferring consumer goods, the maintenance of appearances via servants and a respectable address (Banks, 1981), all of which exerted pressure on family finances and encouraged the rearing of smaller numbers of what economists have called higher-quality children. Even if the middle classes, but especially the lower middle classes of shopkeepers and clerks, were experiencing relative economic pressure in their efforts to attain or retain social respectability and were thus more inclined to plan their families, at least three quarters of Britain's population would conventionally be classified as 'working'. Were there similar pressures on working class couples? It would seem not. Perhaps instead, members of the working class learned from the innovatory class via that group's domestic servants who imparted the ideals and values of the small family rather than the means by which it might be brought about (Banks, 1954).

There is little reason to doubt that economic pressures, whether relative or absolute, played an important part in influencing the decision of many couples to limit their fertility in the late nineteenth century, but what still remains in doubt is why that pressure only took tangible effect in the last quarter of the century and why the secular decline of marital fertility occurred so rapidly that different occupations, status groups and social classes all appeared to be reducing their family sizes at about the same rate and time, although from rather different levels (Stevenson, 1920; Innes, 1938; Woods, 1987; Haines, 1989). The notion of social and indeed spatial diffusion is difficult to sustain with the available evidence.

Of those occupational groups that are relatively easy to

identify, coalminers provide interesting illustrations of the difficulties encountered in developing purely economic explanations of fertility decline (Friedlander, 1973; Haines, 1979). Coalmining districts and families are known to have had higher fertility longer and to have been among the last areas and social groups to attempt family limitation. A commonly held account argues that the income curve for coalminers peaked in the early to mid-twenties; there were few employment opportunities for women; such areas contained a surplus of men; and marriage for women was early and general. The demand for male labour was usually buoyant, but the work was dangerous, accidents and injuries common and often fatal. There was, therefore, little economic incentive, as there was in the lower middle classes, to restrict fertility. But it is also likely that these rather closely knit communities perpetuated an ethos which was strongly orientated towards men's values and women's obligations and thus less compatible with that degree of foresight and co-operation between the sexes necessary for successful family limitation before the development of effective intra-uterine devices and oral contraceptives. (Compare West Lothian and County Durham with the other counties in Tables 5 and 6.)

This leads us on to consider the sociological approach. Here the emphasis is on attitudes and values; the ability of women to negotiate and of men to insist. The process might be thought analogous to a massive and irreversible electoral swing in which there are many polling days, but the results are not immediately obvious. Soon all eligible adults decide to act in the same manner, some copy others, but most make independent decisions based on their own self-interest. If this analogy is close, then it is also necessary to establish what self-interest dictated for most married couples and whether that changed, and also the nature of the constraints on implementation and whether they disappeared in the late nineteenth century. It would seem likely that the balance of costs and returns tipped against large families at an early stage in the process of urban and industrial growth. One might even argue that in such an individualistic society as Britain's, but also one in which the state, as well as the family, had traditionally taken some responsibility for supporting the poor and the old, the investment in children could only be recovered when those children were employed but unmarried (a period of perhaps ten to fifteen years), and not necessarily when the parents were unwell, infirm or aged. In British society, certainly in the eighteenth and nineteenth centuries, children were born and raised 'for their own sakes' rather than for any rationally calculated long-term financial return or insurance. Self-interest should have dictated the practice of moral restraint and direct family limitation by whatever means available among the rich and poor alike. Relative economic pressure felt by the middle classes and the decline of child mortality in the late nineteenth century would have confirmed views on what self-interest should imply.

What were the constraints on behaviour that deflected the attainment of this self-interest? The belief that sexual intercourse was only intended for procreation, and the prevailing moral code of which that was a part, made the question of how many children a married couple should have not only unanswerable, but unthinkable. Children were the gifts of God, and God could only be thwarted by postponing marriage (à la Malthus) or practising a degree of celibacy in marriage. Condoms, widely applied as a prophylactic, were not for use with respectable married women. By the last quarter of the nineteenth century these aspects of the dominant moral code had probably lost their force, partly because the Christian theology on which they were founded had become increasingly more divorced from urban working-class culture, and also because women had become more assertive in their attitude to marital relations. The secularization of nineteenth-century British society accompanied urbanization and can be indexed by the decline in church attendance and the increasing popularity of civil marriage in England and Wales after 1837 (Anderson, O., 1975). For women, the increased involvement in formal education, even before the 1870 Education Act, and the improved literacy are likely to have both caused and symbolised changes in confidence and thus their bargaining power. In the early twentieth century this process also included emancipation and far greater involvement in the non-domestic labour force (Banks and Banks, 1964; Roberts, 1984).

Figure 6 shows one index of marital fertility (I_g) and three other indices of female literacy, living standards and civil marriages. It would be unwise to conclude that merely because the trends in these four indices combine to tell the same story that cause may be inferred, but the story is certainly plausible. In parts of Scotland and much of Ireland high marital fertility persisted into the twentieth century. On the coalfields and north-east Scotland, I_g was still in excess of 0.7 in 1901, but it declined thereafter. In the far north and the Scottish islands marital fertility was also high, but there, like Ireland, nuptiality was at a particularly low level and rates of natural population growth were kept in check. In England and Wales, to which Figure 6 applies, the coalfields were also the most conspicuous areas of persistently high marital fertility, but there too, as with equivalent districts in Scotland, France, Belgium and Germany, attitudes and behaviour eventually came to favour family limitation (Anderson and Morse, 1990; Teitelbaum, 1984; Woods, 1987).

However, it should also be stressed that the British experience of the secular decline of marital fertility was merely part of a Europe-wide movement in which Britain was later than most of France, but in step with much of Germany

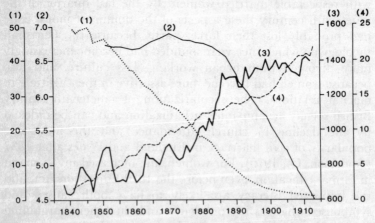

Figure 6 *The percentage of brides signing the marriage register with a mark (1); the index of marital fertility, I_g (2); an index of real wages (3); and the percentage of civil marriages (4) in England and Wales. Source: Woods (1987, 308)*

and Italy (Coale and Watkins, 1986; Watkins, 1991; see also Figure 3). The most important structural barriers to change appear to have been the major linguistic and cultural divisions, as well as the strength of pro-natalist religious feeling. Just as in Britain, it is not possible to say in detail how or why family limitation began to be practised, but the most plausible interpretations also stress the importance of changes in attitude and the removal of constraints on behaviour emphasised in the sociological approach rather than the after effects of industrialization and urbanization or the prior decline of infant and child mortality. The electoral swing was Europe wide, relatively rapid, and has not been reversed.

6 Mortality

The works of two men have come to dominate our
understanding of mortality patterns in the nineteenth
century: William Farr and Thomas McKeown. The former,
as we have already seen, was largely responsible for shaping
the Victorian system of civil registration, while the latter's
account of the course of mortality changes in Britain since the
eighteenth century relied heavily on Farr's legacy of cause of
death reporting. Both were medically trained and perhaps, as
a consequence, they tended to see demographic change
virtually exclusively in terms of mortality, morbidity and
health, to the neglect of other factors. For McKeown, in
particular, the modern rise of population was almost entirely a
matter of mortality decline. Despite the fact that such a view is
demonstrably no longer tenable, the set of arguments with
which McKeown is most closely associated are still worth
careful scrutiny. But before we consider these problems of
interpretation and method, let us first follow Farr and search
for empirical 'laws of mortality'.

Farr himself was occupied with the problem of calculating
accurate English life tables which would not only provide
much-needed material for the life assurance companies to
assess premiums, but would also chart one of the fundamental
'laws of mortality', namely its regular variation with age (Farr,
1864). Figure 7 shows results from two examples of Farr's
work, the 1841 table for Liverpool and the Third English Life
Table for 1838–54, as well as one for Glasgow, 1870–72, and
the Eighth English Life Table for 1910–12 (Woods and Hinde,
1987). The curves show the number of survivors to any age left
from 1,000 live births. They are matched by life expectations
at birth (e_0) and infant mortality rates (IMR) of 26 and 253 for
Liverpool, 32 and 170 for Glasgow, 41 and 149 for ELT 3, 53
and 109 for ELT 8. Mortality was obviously higher in

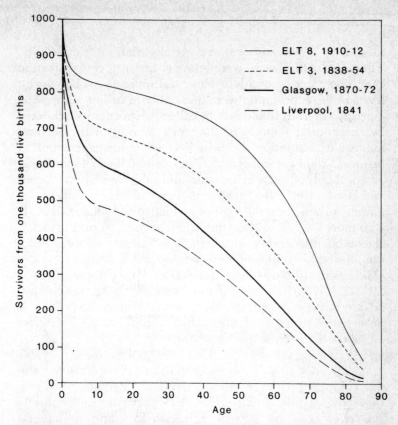

Figure 7 *The numbers surviving to each age out of 1,000 live births.*

Liverpool and Glasgow than England and Wales as a whole; infant and childhood mortality in combination could have been responsible for from 15 to 30 per cent of all deaths, and mortality certainly did decline by at least 20 per cent between mid-century and 1911: these are the three principal findings illustrated in Figure 7.

During the nineteenth century, life expectation at birth in Britain improved from the mid-thirties to the upper forties and the low fifties by 1911. It is now at least 75 years (Table 4 and Figure 2). Of the change, most occurred in the latter part of the nineteenth century and was particularly obvious among those aged from 5 to 25. There was little or no secular decline either in national infant mortality levels or in mortality rates for those aged 35 plus before 1900 (Woods and Woodward, 1984, *39*). But there were important local and social variations in mortality. The local differences were closely tied to environmental conditions, but especially urban/rural differences. The lowest levels of life expectation were invariably in urban places, and especially in what would now be called the inner cities inhabited by the poorest families in the worst housing with the most inadequate sanitation. Even in 1841 when life expectation at birth was 26 in Liverpool and 37 in London, it was 45 in Surrey and probably 50 years in the most salubrious rural areas (Woods and Hinde, 1987). By 1911 the national average had increased and the urban-rural differential had narrowed substantially. It is far more difficult to assess the pattern of occupation and social-class related mortality, although Farr was also responsible for the first tabulations of occupation-specific mortality rates (McDowall, 1983). It remains a matter of speculation whether the wealthy urban middle classes or the poor agricultural labourers experienced the lower level of mortality. Table 7 provides an example of the problems to be resolved. It gives estimates of the class-specific infant mortality rates for 1895–7 and 1910 using the 1911 classification first introduced in Table 2. It shows not only that levels declined for every class, but also that compared with the national trend for England and Wales, they did so at different rates. Class VIII (agricultural labourers) was overtaken by class I (professionals and managers) (Watterson, 1986, 1988). The children of the largely urban middle classes came to fare better than those of the rural working classes.

These are the basic regularities of Victorian mortality which Farr did so much to reveal to his contemporaries: mortality varied with age in a regular fashion (Figure 7); for most ages male mortality was in excess of that for females; strong urban-rural and inner city-suburban contrasts were broadly associated with environmental quality; certain occupations were especially unhealthy, dangerous or accident prone; and mortality rates tended to mirror differences of wealth and social class. Although these often observed regularities assist the search for order, additional perspectives are necessary if the origins and causes of the secular decline in mortality are to be interpreted successfully. It is here that we turn to McKeown, but especially the paper he published with R. G. Record in

58

Table 7 *Estimated Class-Specific Infant Mortality Rates by Father's Social Class for England and Wales*

		1895–7	1910	Change index
I	Professionals	121	59	159
II	Intermediate	138	92	103
III	Skilled workers and clerical	147	97	106
IV	Intermediate	149	105	91
V	Unskilled workers	166	127	72
VI	Textile workers	164	123	78
VII	Miners	169	132	68
VIII	Agricultural labourers	110	87	65

The 1911 classification for I to V is similar to that for 1951, but VI to VIII are dealt with separately (see Table 2).
Change index: $\{[(1895\text{–}7\text{–}1910)/1895\text{–}7]/k\} \times 100$, where k is the equivalent rate of change of national infant mortality between 1895–7 and 1910 (i.e. 0.32).
Source: based on Woods, Watterson and Woodward (1988, *364*)

1962, 'Reasons for the decline of mortality in England and Wales during the nineteenth century', and his 1976 book, *The Modern Rise of Population* (McKeown and Record, 1962; McKeown, 1976). In reading these and other works by McKeown on the same theme it is worth bearing in mind the following points. First, McKeown overemphasized the importance of mortality decline for the modern rise of population in Britain compared with fertility; it is also likely that he over-dramatized the fall in mortality that was particular to the nineteenth century. Secondly, his method of accounting, working backwards from cause of death data to infer the most likely ultimate causes, whether environmental, economic, epidemiological or medical for example, assumes that the data are sound, that there is little need for corroborating evidence and that the contribution of these ultimate causes may thus be quantified. All of these assumptions must be treated with caution. Thirdly, despite these problems, McKeown's central conclusion that, 'with the notable exception of vaccination against smallpox, specific preventive or curative measures could have had no significant influence on mortality before the twentieth century', is still valid (McKeown and Record, 1962, *94*). Fourthly, relatively little notice is taken of the 'laws of mortality' which were apparent to Farr as well as other Victorian medical statisticians, and which have been outlined above (Newsholme, 1889). In particular, McKeown did not disaggregate the pattern of mortality change by region or locality in such a way that the slow decline in rural areas could be contrasted with the more rapid fall from higher levels in the larger cities at the same time that those very cities were housing an increasing share of Britain's population (Woods, 1985; Williamson, 1990).

The critical focus for McKeown's analysis is summarized in Table 8. Over 90 per cent of the late nineteenth-century mortality decline in England and Wales was due to conditions attributable to micro-organisms, with 33 per cent associated

Table 8 *Cause-Specific Standardized Death Rates for England and Wales (figures in parts per million)*

Cause of death	1848–54	1901	1971	Percentage reduction*
A Conditions attributable to micro-organisms				
1 Airborne diseases	7,259	5,122	619	44
2 Water- and food-borne diseases	3,562	1,931	35	33
3 Other conditions	2,144	1,415	60	15
	12,965	8,468	714	92
B Conditions not attributable to micro-organisms	8,891	8,490	4,670	8
Total all diseases	21,865	16,958	5,384	100

* In the period 1848–54 to 1901 and attributable to each category.
Source: McKeown (1976, *54*)

with respiratory tuberculosis; 17 per cent with typhoid and typhus (quite different diseases, but not separated in official statistics until 1869); 12 per cent from cholera, diarrhoea and dysentery; 12 per cent from scarlet fever and diptheria; 5 per cent from smallpox and 4 per cent from non-respiratory tuberculosis. Working backwards from these immediate causes McKeown argued that 'the specific changes introduced by the sanitary reformers were responsible for about a quarter of the total decline of mortality in the second half of the nineteenth century'. The remainder of the improvement, mainly associated with tuberculosis, must be attributed to the rise of living standards brought about by the industrial revolution, that is, 'perhaps half of the total reduction of mortality' (McKeown and Record, 1962, *120*). The last quarter could be attributed to changes in the character of diseases, but especially scarlet fever (Eyler, 1987). The argument for the attribution of the first quarter is relatively easy to follow, how else could the water-borne diseases have declined, but what of tuberculosis? The direct effects of specific therapeutic measures can be ruled out; conditions of exposure to the disease, diet, physical and mental stress remain. McKeown excluded the last-mentioned and claimed that exposure via crowding at home and at work were not reduced before 1900. Thus diet remained the most likely influence on the downward trend of tuberculosis mortality.

Now that we have seen McKeown's full hand, and suspect it to be of variable quality, how might it be strengthened? First, one might seek direct evidence of improvements in living standards, but especially diet, and thereby assess their influence. The available indices of real wages show an upward movement in the second half of the nineteenth century denoting rising living standards which should be associated with improvements in the quantity and quality of food consumed, just as they should with the amelioration of poor housing conditions (Figure 6). However, it is extremely difficult to trace the direct links to their influence, especially on respiratory tuberculosis. Recent efforts in this area have dwelt on problems rather than solutions by stressing the indissolubility of the various influences involved.

The changing nutritional status of Britain's population is

particularly difficult to assess not only because of problems relating to sources, but also the need to select statistical measures that capture both trends in the average position and the relative distribution of experience. The analysis of data on average heights drawn from a wide variety of population samples may help to resolve the matter. Floud, Wachter and Gregory (1990) provide evidence of the steady increase in average heights between 1860 and 1914 which they take to reflect improving nutritional status. The close correlations with rising real wages and falling mortality in this period are also noted. But for the period from 1750 to 1850, when available evidence for real wage and mortality trends are less reliable, data for average heights 'suggests that there was a significant improvement in nutritional status over the whole of the century', and that 'significant inequalities within the working class, as shown by height differentials, narrowed during the late eighteenth and early nineteenth century and then remained roughly constant' (Floud, Wachter and Gregory, 1990, *305*). But the second quarter of the nineteenth century is shown to be a period in which average heights declined, so breaking the long-run trend. Between the 1820s and the 1850s gains in real wages may have been offset by the effects of 'urbanization, diet and possibly work intensity'. The decline of mortality also stabilized or went into reverse during these years (Table 4 and Figure 2). Even if the nutritional status of the British population did improve in the long-term, what implications would this have had for the decline of tuberculosis and the McKeown interpretation in general? How responsive was tuberculosis to improvements in diet? The conclusion to F. B. Smith's study of tuberculosis in the nineteenth century captures the essence of the problem: 'Better nutrition, housing, nurture, lessening of fatigue, smaller family size acting synergistically in varying permu-tations through time and place hold the answer, although that answer remains vague because its chronology and linkages are little traced or understood.' (Smith, 1988, *244*)

Further efforts in this area should probably begin by re-examining the contribution of tuberculosis decline to the fall of mortality.

Secondly, one might look more closely at local variations in mortality decline and consider the way in which the mortality gradient between urban and rural places began to narrow by the early years of the twentieth century (Pelling, 1978; Szreter, 1988). Certainly this aspect was neglected by McKeown, but it too is not free from the problems that are always to be encountered in the analysis of multivariate associations. The urbanization of Britain's population had important consequences for public health, but it also meant that once the technology for sanitary engineering became available, and the need for a constant supply of pure water and effective sewerage recognised, then investment could bring direct and immediate benefits to large numbers very quickly. Once the investment had been made, the carriage systems put in place; the streets cleaned, paved and lighted, and the worst slums swept away; then one's expectations of material advances in health and mortality should certainly be raised. But these investments were the results of political decisions and attitudes which came in a slow and halting fashion to recognise public health as a priority for direct intervention by national and local government (Wohl, 1983; Woods, 1991). The story of how public health became a priority and its rise on the political agenda is intriguing in its own right, for it reflects the combination of initiatives made by individuals (Sir Edwin Chadwick, Dr John Snow and Sir John Simon, for example) as well as changes in attitude among the political elite and their supporters. The latter were influenced by, on the one hand, the successive extension of the electoral franchise and, on the other, by self-interest. Public opinion also came to see the value of direct state intervention, collective action and regulation. Even members of the medical profession played an increasingly confident and interventionist role, especially through the army of Medical Officers of Health which constituted a local health bureaucracy (Frazer, 1947; Hardy, 1988).

The implications for that one quarter of the mortality decline in the last half of the nineteenth century attributed by McKeown to the sanitary reformers are several in number. Above all the course of the sanitary revolution was politically motivated; it did not always take notice of need and was often confounded by vested interest. Certainly reformers did make important contributions, especially in the moulding of public opinion, but the process of change was far wider and probably owed less to inspired individuals than to political expediency in the face of overwhelming evidence for the hazards to health of poor hygiene coupled with growing technical competence (Hassan, 1985; Kearns, 1985).

Thirdly, it may also prove instructive to consider those aspects of the 'laws of mortality' which do not appear to have altered substantially in the nineteenth century. The most obvious example must surely be the persistently high rate of infant mortality (Woods, Watterson and Woodward, 1988–89). In the late nineteenth century between 15 and 20 per cent of deaths in Britain occurred to those under the age of one year with about 25 per cent for those under five years. National trends showed little sign of continued decline until the late 1890s or 1900. Variations between urban and rural places were clear and persistent, with the former two to two and a half times the latter at the extremes, as were the rates related to father's occupation and thereby social class (Table 7). The mortality of infants born to unmarried mothers was substantially higher than that of legitimate children and roughly one third of all infant deaths occurred during the first month of life.

These regularities were all well known to contemporaries and became the subject of particular concern during the 1890s and 1900s when the health of the population, but especially mothers and young children, was the subject of much debate. Sir George Newman's *Infant Mortality: A Social Problem* (1906) set the scene and the tone of where the causes of persistently high infant mortality should be sought. But it was probably the work of Sir Arthur Newsholme, while Medical Officer of Health for Brighton (1888–1908) and Medical Officer of the Local Government Board (1909–19), that most helped to lay a sound foundation for the analysis of infant mortality variations and changes (Newsholme, 1889).

Table 9 arranges the factors suggested by Newsholme in a convenient form. Newsholme, himself, was particularly concerned with the sanitary environment and epidemic diarrhoea which in summer months had been an important, yet avoidable, cause of infant deaths, especially in poor urban environments. In the 1890s diarrhoea appeared to emphasise

64

Table 9 *Influences on Infant Mortality*

	Care		
(A) Mother	**(B)** Of mother	**(C)** Of child	**(D)** Poverty
Age	Ante-natal	Delivery	Housing
Work	Post-natal	(midwifery)	Unemployment
Family	Maternal	Visiting	Wife's work
size	mortality	(care, advice)	Other
Legitimacy		Feeding	children's work
		(i) breast	
		(ii) artificial	
		-form	
		-preparation	

(E) Housing	**(F)** Sanitary environment	**(G)** Personal factors
Type	Pure water	
Crowding	Excreta	
	removal	
	Scavenging	
	Paving	

Source: Woods, Watterson and Woodward (1989, *114*)

the need for further sanitary improvements at a time when general infant mortality rates were rising, even though non-diarrhoeal infant mortality rates were already in decline. Much was also made at the time of the movement away from breastfeeding to the use of artificial feeds and the involvement of mothers in the non-domestic labour force (Dyhouse, 1978; Smith, 1979; Dwork, 1987).

However, it is unlikely that sewerage alone could have made the difference. Mortality among two, three and four year olds was already in decline from the 1870s at least, perhaps partly as a result of changes in disease patterns normally associated with scarlet fever. It is very difficult to chart in any generalized form changes in the practice of infant and child care during this period. What evidence there is suggests that infants were usually breastfed, unless their mothers were physiologically unable, for six or seven months, but that artificial foods did become more popular during the first half of the twentieth century and that many babies experienced a mixed diet of breastmilk and other solids. The evidence on advances in obstetric, ante- and post-natal care is similarly ambiguous. The training and registration of midwives certainly improved in the 1900s and many local authorities established clinics for maternal and child care, but neonatal mortality changed very little at 40 to 50 per thousand live births throughout the 1890s, 1900s and 1910s, and maternal mortality also stayed remarkably constant until the 1930s (Loudon, 1988). It would seem that if child-care practices did improve then the beneficiaries were infants aged one month and older.

The role of fertility decline must also be considered at this point (Reves, 1985). Certainly the reduction in illegitimate births would have depleted the most at-risk category of infants, but it is also reasonable to expect that efforts at family limitation not only reduced the sizes of completed families, but also served to lengthen the intervals between births rather more. Mothers would have been able to provide better care for fewer children and, if birth intervals were also increased to three, four or more years, the problem of competition for care between very young siblings would also have been avoided. If this outline is valid then we are left to ask once again, what caused the decline of fertility in late nineteenth-century Britain? Of the various factors already reviewed, the improvement in standards of education, but especially those of women, would seem of special significance not only for family limitation, but also the possibility of child care training via special literature, by nurses and health visitors (Woods, Watterson and Woodward, 1988–89).

All of this is highly speculative yet the story it suggests is credible and complements a similar one emerging in Third World countries. Fertility control programmes work most effectively when they operate alongside schemes to improve maternal and child health. In Britain the control of fertility, by whatever means, probably helped to initiate the decline of infant mortality, a connection obscured by high rates of diarrhoeal infant mortality in the 1890s, but the secular decline was reinforced by improving urban sanitation and eventually better obstetric facilities and targeted child health care programmes.

The course of infant mortality decline suggests certain implications for the fall of mortality in general and the manner in which McKeown's interpretation may be extended. First, it reinforces the need to search for connections between a wide range of factors which may not only support, or even amplify each other's contribution, but may also operate in a sequential fashion so that their relative importance will change over a period of several decades. Secondly, it emphasises the benefits of tracing temporal changes in a disaggregated fashion which allows for regional, local and social trends to emerge. But it also highlights the danger of generalizing from the experience of just one age group, for infant mortality was not only of special significance for the rise of life expectation at birth, its secular decline also followed a separate and rather distinctive course.

Farr's tireless work on the vital statistics of England and Wales have made it possible to describe in some detail the pattern of mortality variation in the nineteenth century, but we are still some way off providing a full explanation of the origins of the secular decline of mortality during the nineteenth century. We know that medical science could have had only a minor influence on the decline of mortality before the 1930s and that the cleansing of great cities was a special problem in a country like Great Britain which had a particularly high level of urbanization, but once the sanitation and public health problem in general had been solved then the positive effects would have been immediate and lasting. We also know that poverty, poor diet and thus low nutritional status, and inadequate housing persisted and were then, as now, closely related to variations in mortality rates. The significance of and reasons for the decline of mortality from tuberculosis continues to be an area for enquiry, but few now follow McKeown's lead and argue from mortality via tuberculosis to improved living standards, especially diet. Few would be bold enough to attach precise weights to the various factors apparently in operation. Many would now regard the nineteenth century as a period in which the foundations of modern medical science were laid, but that most of the fruits have only been available in this century (Pickstone, 1985).

7 1911

If Malthus had returned to survey Britain's population in 1911 he would have been struck by its size, the extent of its concentration in large towns and the apparently effortless way in which real wages had been rising in recent decades. Misery and vice were still in evidence, moral restraint was practised, but new forms of restraint were used by married couples to limit their fertility. Differences in health and mortality between urban and rural environments and social classes persisted, but the former at least had recently shown marked signs of narrowing as the urban penalty weakened under the influence of public health reforms. Malthus would also have been shocked by Ireland's experience and at the state of the workhouses. He would have enjoyed the wealth of new statistics and been frustrated by their lacunae. Finally, he would probably have been startled by the pace not only of demographic change, but also of politics, the economy and society, and would doubtless have been apprehensive about what the future held in store now that some of the old certainties had lost their meaning.

The year 1911 is a convenient one with which to close. It was a census year and one with a hot, dry summer which tested public health to the limit. It was also the year in which the English and Welsh local authorities became the new units for civil registration. By 1911 the secular decline of both mortality and fertility, even infant mortality, were well underway and largely irreversible. The age of great cities had not yet yielded to the motor car and the long-distance commuter train, to counter-urbanization and *urbs in rure*, nor had slum clearance depopulated the inner city so completely. There were horses in the fields, bicycles in the lanes; but women feared pregnancy as the old did the workhouse, and more than one in ten babies died before reaching their first birthday.

Certainly our understanding of these phenomena has improved considerably in recent years, largely because we now have estimates of demographic indices of periods before the first population census was taken and civil registration was introduced, at least in England, and can determine how the modern rise of population occurred. There is also some indication that old sources are being put to better effect using large databases and computer-assisted nominal record linkage. Single-discipline perspectives are also becoming less popular as historians and social scientists attempt to develop a common language. For the historical demography of the nineteenth century this will mean the integration of space with time and greater emphasis on the interaction between migration, fertility and mortality, environment and social class.

If the conundrum of English population growth in the eighteenth century has been resolved (Wrigley, 1983b), what remains of its nineteenth-century equivalent for Great Britain? The so-called McKeown problem has not yet been solved in the absence of a satisfactory method of ascribing numerical influence to those factors affecting mortality decline. Without reliable information on the means by which family limitation was brought about and a strategy for inferring motivation, the fertility transition will ultimately remain the subject for speculation in the absence of adequate evidence. The conflict between the free will of individuals and their obligation to conform to group social norms is still an intriguing issue in the study of migration, marriage and fertility control. The need to maintain a consciously comparative perspective also remains pressing and thereby to place Britain's demographic experience in a wider international context.

When the late M. W. Flinn completed his pamphlet on the population of eighteenth-century Britain in 1970 much still remained obscure. Now the course of English population history is reasonably clear. Equivalent substantial advances in our understanding of the processes and causes of demographic change in the nineteenth century are possible in the years to come, but they are most likely to stem from more imaginative use of familiar sources, the release of new material and above all the ability of scholars to think beyond the bounds set by disciplines back into the minds of their Georgian and Victorian ancestors.

Glossary of Demographic Terms

Although readers should refer to Roland Pressat's *Dictionary of Demography* (edited by Christopher Wilson, Oxford, 1986) for more detailed information of demographic terms, a brief introduction may prove useful.

Crude rates – live births (crude birth rate, CBR) or deaths (crude death rate, CDR) per 1,000 population (e.g. Table 4)

Infant mortality rate – infant deaths (under one year of age) per 1,000 live births in a year (e.g. Tables 4 and 7)

Princeton or A. J. Coale's fertility indices (Coale and Watkins, 1986) – the four indices are overall fertility (I_f), marital fertility (I_g), illegitimate fertility (I_h) and proportion married (I_m). They are indirectly standardized measures which use the marital fertility of Hutterite women married 1921–30 (Figure 4) as their standard against which to estimate the expected number of births with which the actual is then compared. They enable the influence of variations in age structures and marriage patterns to be taken into account even where age-specific marital fertility cannot be calculated directly (e.g. Table 4, 5 and 6, Figure 6). The indices are related in the following way:

$$I_f = I_m \text{ x } I_g + I_h (1 - I_m)$$

and if I_h is zero then $I_f = I_m$ x I_g (Figure 5 uses this property to construct the curved isolines for I_f).

Gross reproduction rate (GRR) – the average number of daughters that would be born to a woman during her lifetime if she passed through the childbearing ages experiencing the average age-specific fertility pattern of a given period, often a year (Figures 2 and 3).

Age-specific marital fertility – the number of legitimate births per 1,000 married women by five-year age groups (e.g. Figure 4)

Natural fertility – that fertility which is not influenced by deliberate attempts at that form of family limitation which takes account of the number of previous live births, that is fertility which is not the subject of parity-specific control

Life tables – a system for expressing the probability of dying by age, survivorship (Figure 7) and life expectation at age x (e_x)

Life expectation at birth (e_0) – the average number of years a newly-born baby may be expected to live (Table 4 and Figures 2 and 3).

Intrinsic rate of natural population growth (r) – the annual rate at which a closed stable population grows when it is not affected by migration. Figure 3 has been so constructed to reveal the changing contribution of fertility (via GRR) and mortality (via e_0) to r.

Bibliography

The bibliography is arranged in sections that relate to the seven chapters. Material referred to in each chapter will be listed in that chapter's section along with other useful items. The bibliography begins with some of the most valuable general references.

General references

Anderson, M. (1988a) *Population Change in North-Western Europe, 1750–1850* (London).
Deane, P. and Cole, W. A. (1967) *British Economic Growth* (Cambridge).
Flinn, M. W. (1970) *British Population Growth 1700–1850* (London).
Flinn, M. W. (ed) (1977) *Scottish Population History: From the Seventeenth Century to the 1930s* (Cambridge).
Flinn, M. W. (1981) *The European Demographic System, 1500–1820* (Brighton).
Fraser, W. H. and Morris, R. J. (eds) (1990) *People and Society in Scotland, Volume II, 1830–1914* (Edinburgh).
Smout, T. C. (1986) *A Century of the Scottish People, 1830–1950* (London).
Thompson, F. M. L. (ed) (1990) *The Cambridge Social History of Britain, 1750–1950 Volume 2: People and their Environment* (Cambridge).
Wrigley, E. A. (1987) *People, Cities and Wealth* (Oxford).
Wrigley, E. A. (1988) *Continuity, Chance and Change* (Cambridge).
Wrigley, E. A. and Schofield, R. S. (1981) *The Population History of England, 1541–1871: A Reconstruction* (London; Cambridge, 1989).

Chapter 1 – Malthus's Britain

Anderson, M. (1988a) *Population Change in North-Western Europe, 1750–1850* (London).

Coleman, D. and Schofield, R. S. (eds) (1986) *The State of Population Theory: Forward from Malthus* (Oxford).

Macfarlane, A. (1986) *Marriage and Love in England, 1300–1840* (Oxford).

Malthus, T. R. (1798 and 1803) *An Essay on the Principle of Population* (First edition (1798) edited by A. Flew, Harmondsworth, 1970; Second (1803) and subsequent editions edited by P. James, Cambridge, 1989).

Wilson, C. and Woods, R. I. (1992) 'Fertility in England: a long-term perspective' *Population Studies* 46.

Wrigley, E. A. (1983a) 'Malthus's model of a pre-industrial economy' in J. Dupâquier and A. Fauve-Chamoux (eds) *Malthus Past and Present* (London), pp. 111–24.

Wrigley, E. A. (1983b) 'The growth of population in eighteenth-century England: a conundrum resolved' *Past and Present* 98, pp. 121–50.

Wrigley, E. A. (1988) *Continuity, Chance and Change* (Cambridge)

Wrigley, E. A. and Schofield, R.S. (1981) *The Population History of England, 1541–1871: A Reconstruction* (London; Cambridge, 1989).

Chapter 2 – What do we know and how do we know it?

Anderson, M. (1985) 'The emergence of the modern life cycle in Britain' *Social History* 10, pp. 69–87.

Anderson, M. (1990) 'The social implications of demographic change' in F. M. L. Thompson (ed) *The Cambridge Social History of Britain, 1750–1950. Volume 2: People and their Environment* (Cambridge), pp. 1–70.

Armstrong, W. A. (1974) *Stability and Change in an English County Town: A Social Study of York, 1801–51* (Cambridge).

Armstrong, W. A. (1981) 'The flight from the land' in G. E. Mingay (ed) *The Victorian Countryside* (London), pp. 118–35.

Banks, J. A. (1978) 'The social structure of nineteenth century England as seen through the census' in R. Lawton (ed) *The Census and Social Structure* (London), pp. 179–223.

Craig, J. (1987) 'Changes in the population composition of England and Wales since 1841' *Population Trends* 48, pp. 27–36.

Eyler, J. M. (1979) *Victorian Social Medicine: The Ideas and Methods of William Farr* (Baltimore).

Farr, W. (1864) *English Life Tables. Tables of Lifetimes, Annuities, and Premiums* (London).

Farr, W. (1885) *Vital Statistics* (London).

Glass, D. V. (1951) 'A note on the under-registration of births in Britain in the nineteenth century' *Population Studies* 5, pp. 70–88.

Hewitt, M. (1958) *Wives and Mothers in Victorian Industry* (London).

Higgs, E. (1989) *Making Sense of the Census: The Manuscript Returns for England and Wales, 1801–1901*, Public Record Office Handbooks No. 23 (London).

Hinde, P. R. A. (1987) 'The population of a Wiltshire village in the nineteenth century: a reconstitution study of Berwick St James, 1841–71' *Annals of Human Biology* 14, pp. 475–85.

Law, C. M. (1967) 'The growth of urban population in England and Wales, 1801–1911' *Transactions of the Institute of British Geographers* 41, pp. 125–43.

Lawton, R. (1958) 'Population movements in the West Midlands, 1841–1861' *Geography* 43, pp. 164–77.

Lawton, R. (1972) 'An age of great cities' *Town Planning Review* 43, pp. 199–224.

Lawton, R. (ed) (1978) *The Census and Social Structure: An Interpretive Guide to Nineteenth Century Censuses for England and Wales* (London).

Lawton, R. (1983) 'Urbanization and population change in nineteenth-century England' in J.Patten (ed) *The Expanding City* (London), pp. 179–224.

Laxton, P. (1981) 'Liverpool in 1801: a manuscript return for the first national census' *Transactions of the Historic Society of Lancashire and Cheshire* 130, pp. 73–113.

Lee, R. D. and Lam, D. (1983) 'Age distribution adjustments for English censuses, 1821 to 1931' *Population Studies* 37, pp. 445–64.

Malthus, T. R. (1803) *An Essay on the Principals of Population* (Second edn ed. by P. James, Cambridge, 1989).

Mitchell, B. R. (1988) *British Historical Statistics* (Cambridge).

Newsholme, A. (1889) *The Elements of Vital Statistics* (London).

Nissel, M. (1987) *People Count: A History of the General Register Office* (London).

Roberts, E. (1984) *A Woman's Place: An Oral History of Working-Class Women, 1890–1940* (Oxford).

Routh, G. (1987) *Occupations of the People of Great Britain, 1801–1981* (London).

Szreter, S. R. S. (1984) 'The genesis of the Registrar-General's social classification of occupations' *British Journal of Sociology* 35, pp. 522–46.

Teitelbaum, M. S. (1974) 'Birth under-registration in the constituent counties of England and Wales, 1841–1910' *Population Studies* 28, pp. 329–43.

Weber, A. F. (1899) *The Growth of Cities in the Nineteenth Century: A Study in Statistics* (New York; Ithaca, 1963).

Welton, T. A. (1911) *England's Recent Progress: An Investigation of the Statistics of Migrations, Mortality, etc in the Twenty Years from 1881–1901* (London).

Wrigley, E. A. (ed) (1966) *An Introduction to English Historical Demography* (London).

Wrigley, E. A. (ed) (1972) *Nineteenth Century Society: Essays in the Use of Quantitative Methods for the Study of Social Data* (Cambridge).

Chapter 3 – Whether to stay and where to go

Anderson, M. and Morse, D. (1990) 'The people' in W.H. Fraser and R.J. Morris (eds) *People and Society in Scotland Volume II, 1830–1914* (Edinburgh), pp. 8–45.

Baines, D. (1985) *Migration in a Mature Economy: Emigration and Internal Migration in England and Wales, 1861–1900* (Cambridge).

Carrier, N. H. and Jeffery, J. R. (1953) *External Migration: A Study of the Available Statistics, 1815–1950*, Studies on Medical and Population Subjects No. 6 (London).

Cairncross, A. K. (1953) 'Internal migration in Victorian England' in *Home and Foreign Investment, 1870–1913* (Cambridge), pp. 65–83.

Dennis, R.J. (1984) *English Industrial Cities of the Nineteenth*

Century (Cambridge).

Easterlin, R. A. (1961) 'Influences on European overseas emigration before World War I' *Economic Development and Cultural Change* 9, pp. 331–51.

Flinn, M. W. (ed) (1977) *Scottish Population History: From the Seventeenth Century to the 1930s* (Cambridge).

Friedlander, D. and Roshier, D. J. (1966) 'A study of internal migration in England and Wales' *Population Studies* 19, pp. 239–79 and 20, pp. 45–59.

Grigg, D.B. (1977) 'E. G. Ravenstein and the laws of migration' *Journal of Historical Geography* 3, pp. 41–54.

Kearns, G. and Withers, C. W. J. (eds) (1991) *Urbanizing Britain* (Cambridge).

Law, C. M. (1967) 'The growth of urban population in England and Wales, 1801–1911' *Transactions of the Institute of British Geographers* 41, pp. 125–43.

Lawton, R. (1956) 'The population of Liverpool in the mid-nineteenth century' *Transactions of the Historic Society of Lancashire and Cheshire* 107, pp. 89–120.

Lawton, R. (1959) 'Irish migration to England and Wales in the mid-nineteenth century' *Irish Geography* 4, pp. 35–54.

Lawton, R. (1967) 'Rural depopulation in nineteenth-century England' in R.W.Steel and R. Lawton (eds) *Liverpool Essays in Geography* (London), pp. 227–55.

Lawton, R. (1968) 'Population changes in England and Wales in the later nineteenth century: an analysis of trends by registration districts' *Transactions of the Institute of British Geographers* 44, pp. 55–74.

Lawton, R. (1979) 'Mobility in nineteenth–century British cities' *Geographical Journal* 145, pp. 206–24.

Lawton, R. (1983) 'Urbanization and population change in nineteenth-century England' in J.Patten (ed) *The Expanding City* (London), pp. 179–224.

Lees, L. H. (1979) *Exiles of Erin: Irish Emigrants in Victorian London* (Ithaca).

Morris, R. J. (1990) 'Urbanization in Scotland' in W. H. Fraser and R. J. Morris (eds) *People and Society in Scotland Volume II, 1830–1914* (Edinburgh), pp. 73–102.

Perry, P. J. (1969) 'Working class isolation and mobility in rural Dorset, 1837–1936: a study of marriage distances'

Transactions of the Institute of British Geographers 46, pp. 115–35.

Pooley, C. G. (1979) 'Residential mobility in the Victorian city' *Transactions of the Institute of British Geographers, New Series* 4, pp. 258–77.

Pooley, C. G. (1983) 'Welsh migrants to England in the mid-nineteenth century' *Journal of Historical Geography* 9, pp. 287–306.

Ravenstein, E. G. (1885 and 1889) 'The laws of migration' *Journal of the Royal Statistical Society* 48, pp. 167–227 and 52, pp. 241–301.

Redford, A. (1926) *Labour Migration in England, 1800–1850* (Manchester).

Saville, J. (1957) *Rural Depopulation in England and Wales, 1851–1951* (London).

Swift, R. and Gilley, S. (eds) (1985) *The Irish in the Victorian City* (London).

Thomas, B. (1954) *Migration and Economic Growth: A Study of Great Britain and the Atlantic Economy* (Cambridge).

Weber, A. F. (1899) *The Growth of Cities in the Nineteenth Century: A Study in Statistics* (New York; Ithaca, 1963).

Withers, C. W. J. and Watson, A. J. (1991) 'Stepwise migration and Highland migration to Glasgow, 1852–1898' *Journal of Historical Geography* 17, pp. 35–55.

Chapter 4 – Marriage

Anderson, M. (1971) *Family Structure in 19th Century Lancashire* (Cambridge).

Anderson, M. (1976) 'Marriage patterns in Victorian Britain: an analysis based on registration district data for England and Wales, 1861' *Journal of Family History* 1, pp. 55–78.

Anderson, M. (1978) 'Sociological history and the working-class family' *Social History* 3, pp. 317–34.

Anderson, M. (1980) *Approaches to the History of the Western Family, 1500–1914* (London).

Anderson, M. (1984) 'The social position of spinsters in mid-Victorian Britain' *Journal of Family History* 9, pp. 377–93.

Anderson, M. (1988b) 'Households, families and individuals: some preliminary results from the national sample from the

1851 census' *Continuity and Change* 3, pp. 421–38.

Anderson, M. and Morse, D. (1990) 'The people' in W.H. Fraser and R.J. Morris (eds) *People and Society in Scotland Volume II, 1830–1914* (Edinburgh), pp. 8–45.

Anderson, O. (1975) 'The incidence of civil marriage in Victorian England and Wales' *Past and Present* 69, pp. 50–87 and 84, pp. 155–62.

Coale, A.J. and Watkins, S.C. (eds) (1986) *The Decline of Fertility in Europe* (Princeton).

Crafts, N.F.R. (1978) 'Average age at first marriage for women in mid-nineteenth century England and Wales: a cross-sectional study' *Population Studies* 32, pp. 21–25.

Friedlander, D. (1973) 'Demographic patterns and socio-economic characteristics of the coal-mining population in England and Wales in the nineteenth century' *Economic Development and Cultural Change* 22, pp. 39–51.

Garrett, E.M. (1990) 'The trials of labour: motherhood versus employment in a nineteenth-century textile centre' *Continuity and Change* 5, pp. 121–54.

Hewitt, M. (1958) *Wives and Mothers in Victorian Industry* (London).

Higgs, E. (1983) 'Domestic servants and households in Victorian England' *Social History* 8, pp. 201–10.

Hinde, P.R.A. (1985) 'Household structure, marriage and the institution of service in nineteenth-century rural England' *Local Population Studies* 35, pp. 43–51.

Hinde, P.R.A. (1989) 'The marriage market in the nineteenth-century English countryside' *European Journal of Economic History* 18, pp. 383–92.

Kabir, M. (1980) 'Regional variations in nuptiality in England and Wales during the demographic transition' *Genus* 36, pp. 171–87.

Leneman, L. and Mitchison, R. (1987) 'Scottish illegitimacy rates in the early modern period' *Economic History Review, 2nd Series* 40, pp. 41–63.

Litchfield, R.B. (1988) 'Single people in the nineteenth-century city: a comparative perspective on occupations and living situations' *Continuity and Change* 3, pp. 83–100.

Mitchison, R. and Leneman, L. (1989) *Sexuality and Social Control: Scotland, 1660–1780* (Oxford).

Ogle, W. (1890) 'On marriage rates and marriage ages, with special reference to the growth of population' *Journal of the Royal Statistical Society* 53, pp. 253–80.

Stone, L. (1990) *Road to Divorce: England, 1530–1987* (Oxford)

Tranter, N. L. (1985) 'Illegitimacy in nineteenth century rural Scotland. A puzzle resolved' *International Journal of Sociology and Social Policy* 5, pp. 33–46.

Wall, R., Robin, J. and Laslett, P. (eds) (1983) *Family Forms in Historic Europe* (Cambridge).

Wilson, C. and Woods, R.I. (1992) 'Fertility in England: a long-term perspective' *Population Studies* 46.

Woods, R.I. (1984) 'Social class variations in the decline of marital fertility in late nineteenth-century London' *Geografiska Annaler* 66B, pp. 29–38.

Woods, R.I. (1992) 'What happened to the preventive check in late nineteenth-century England?' in R.M. Smith (ed) *Demographic Patterns in the Past* (Oxford).

Woods, R.I. and Hinde, P.R.A. (1985) 'Nuptiality and age at marriage in nineteenth-century England' *Journal of Family History* 10, pp. 119–44.

Chapter 5 – How many children should we have?

Anderson, M. and Morse, D. (1990) 'The people' in W.H. Fraser and R.J.Morris (eds) *People and Society in Scotland Volume II, 1830–1914* (Edinburgh), pp. 8–45.

Anderson, O. (1975) 'The incidence of civil marriage in Victorian England and Wales' *Past and Present* 69, pp. 50–87 and 84, pp. 155–62.

Banks, J.A. (1954) *Prosperity and Parenthood: A Study of Family Planning Among the Victorian Middle Classes* (London).

Banks, J.A. (1981) *Victorian Values: Secularism and the Size of Families* (London).

Banks, J.A. and Banks, O. (1964) *Feminism and Family Planning in Victorian England* (Liverpool).

Bongaarts, J. and Potter, R.J. (1983) *Fertility, Biology and Behaviour: An Analysis of the Proximate Determinants* (New York).

Brass, W. and Kabir, M. (1980) 'Regional variations in fertility and child mortality during the demographic transition in England and Wales' in J. Hobcraft and P.H.

Rees (eds) *Regional Demographic Development* (London), pp. 71–88.

Coale, A. J. and Watkins, S. C. (eds) (1986) *The Decline of Fertility in Europe* (Princeton).

Crafts, N. F. R. (1984a) 'A time series study of fertility in England and Wales, 1877–1938' *European Journal of Economic History* 13, pp. 571–90.

Crafts, N. F. R. (1984b) 'A cross-sectional study of legitimate fertility in England and Wales, 1911' *Research in Economic History* 9, pp. 89–107.

Davies, M. (1982) 'Corsets and conception: fashion and demographic trends in the nineteenth century' *Comparative Studies in Society and History* 24, pp. 611–41.

Friedlander, D. (1973) 'Demographic patterns and socio-economic characteristics of the coal-mining population in England and Wales in the nineteenth century' *Economic Development and Cultural Change* 22, pp. 39–51.

Garrett, E. M. (1990) 'The trials of labour: motherhood versus employment in a nineteenth-century textile centre' *Continuity and Change* 5, pp. 121–54.

Glass, D. V. (1938) 'Changes in fertility in England and Wales, 1851–1931' In L. Hogben (ed) *Political Arithmetic* (London), pp. 161–212.

Haines, M. R. (1979) *Fertility and Occupation: Population Patterns in Industrialization* (New York).

Haines, M. R. (1989) 'Social class differentials during fertility decline: England and Wales revisited' *Population Studies* 43, pp. 305–22.

Hinde, P. R. A. and Woods, R. I. (1984) 'Variations in historical natural fertility patterns and the measurement of fertility control' *Journal of Biosocial Science* 16, pp. 309–21.

Innes, J. W. (1938) *Class Fertility Trends in England and Wales, 1876–1934* (Princeton).

Litchfield, R. B. (1978) 'The family and the mill: cottonmill work, family work patterns and fertility in mid-Victorian Stockport' in A. S. Wohl (ed) *The Victorian Family* (London), pp. 180–96.

McLaren, A. (1977) 'Women's work and the regulation of family size' *History Workshop Journal* 4, pp. 70–81.

McLaren, A. (1978) *Birth Control in Nineteenth-Century England*

(London).

Newsholme, A. and Stevenson, T. H. C. (1906) 'The decline of human fertility in the United Kingdom and other countries as shown by corrected birth rates' *Journal of the Royal Statistical Society* 69, pp. 34–87.

Peel, J. (1963) 'The manufacture and retailing of contraceptives in England' *Population Studies* 17, pp. 113–25.

Reves, R. (1985) 'Declining fertility in England and Wales as a major cause of the twentieth century decline in mortality: the role of changing family size and age structure in infectious disease mortality in infancy' *American Journal of Epidemiology* 122, pp. 112–26.

Roberts, E. (1984) *A Woman's Place: An Oral History of Working-Class Women, 1890–1940* (Oxford).

Sauer, R. (1978) 'Infanticide and abortion in nineteenth century Britain' *Population Studies* 32, pp. 81–93.

Seccombe, W. (1990) 'Starting to stop: working-class fertility decline in Britain' *Past and Present* 126, pp. 151–88.

Shorter, E. (1973) 'Female emancipation, birth control and fertility in European history' *American Historical Review* 78, pp. 605–40.

Soloway, R. A. (1982) *Birth Control and the Population Question in England, 1877–1930* (Chapel Hill).

Stevenson, T. H. C. (1920) 'The fertility of various social classes in England and Wales from the middle of the nineteenth century to 1911' *Journal of the Royal Statistical Society* 83, pp. 401–32.

Teitelbaum, M. S. (1984) *The British Fertility Decline: Demographic Transition in the Crucible of the Industrial Revolution* (Princeton).

Watkins, S. C. (1991) *From Provinces to Nations: Demographic Integration in Western Europe, 1870–1960* (Princeton).

Wilson, C. (1984) 'Natural fertility in pre-industrial England' *Population Studies* 38, pp. 225–40.

Wilson, C. (1986) 'The proximate determinants of marital fertility in England, 1600–1899' in L. Bonfield, R. M. Smith and K. Wrightson (eds) *The World We Have Gained* (Oxford), pp. 203–30.

Wilson, C. and Woods, R. I. (1992) 'Fertility in England: a long-term perspective' *Population Studies* 46.

Woods, R. I. (1987) 'Approaches to the fertility transition in Victorian England' *Population Studies* 41, pp. 283–311.

Woods, R. I. and Smith, C. W. (1983) 'The decline of marital fertility in the late nineteenth century: the case of England and Wales' *Population Studies* 37, pp. 207–25.

Woods, R. I., Watterson, P. A. and Woodward, J. H. (1988–89) 'The causes of rapid infant mortality decline in England and Wales, 1861–1921. Parts I and II' *Population Studies* 42, pp. 343–66 and 43, pp. 113–32.

Chapter 6 – Mortality

Anderson, O. (1987) *Suicide in Victorian England* (Oxford).

Dwork, D. (1987) 'The milk option: an aspect of the history of infant welfare movement in England, 1898–1908' *Medical History* 31, pp. 51–69.

Dyhouse, C. (1978) 'Working-class mothers and infant mortality in England, 1895–1914' *Journal of Social History* 12(2), pp. 248–67.

Eyler, J. M. (1976) 'Mortality statistics and Victorian health policy: program and criticism' *Bulletin of the History of Medicine* 50, pp. 335–55.

Eyler, J. M. (1979) *Victorian Social Medicine: The Ideas and Methods of William Farr* (Baltimore).

Eyler, J. M. (1987) 'Scarlet fever and confinement: the Edwardian debate over isolation hospitals' *Bulletin of the History of Medicine* 61, pp. 1–24.

Farr, W. (1864) *English Life Table. Tables of Lifetimes, Annuities, and Premiums* (London).

Floud, R., Wachter, K. and Gregory, A. (1990) *Height, Health and History: Nutritional Status in the United Kingdom, 1750–1980* (Cambridge).

Frazer, W. M. (1947) *Duncan of Liverpool: An Account of the Work of Dr W. H. Duncan Medical Officer of Health of Liverpool, 1847–63* (London).

Hardy, A. (1983) 'Smallpox in London: Factors in the decline of the disease in the nineteenth century' *Medical History* 27, pp. 111–38.

Hardy, A. (1988) 'Public health and the expert: the London Medical Officers of Health, 1856–1900' in R. MacLeod (ed)

Government and Expertise: Specialists, Administrators and Professionals, 1860–1919 (Cambridge), pp.128–42.

Hassan, J. A. (1985) 'The growth and impact of the British water industry in the nineteenth century' *Economic History Review, 2nd Series* 38, pp. 531–47.

Kearns, G. (1985) *Urban Epidemics and Historical Geography: Cholera in London, 1848–9*, Historical Geography Research Series No. 15 (Norwich).

Kearns, G. (1988) 'Private property and public health reform in England, 1830–1870' *Social Science and Medicine* 26, pp. 187–99.

Kearns, G. (1991) 'Class, biology and the urban penalty' in G. Kearns and C. W. J. Withers (eds) *Urbanizing Britain* (Cambridge).

Lee, C. H. (1991) 'Regional inequalities in infant mortality in Britain, 1861–1971: patterns and hypotheses' *Population Studies* 45, pp. 55–65.

Logan, W. P. D. (1950) 'Mortality in England and Wales from 1848–1947' *Population Studies* 4, pp. 132–78.

Loudon, I. (1986) 'Deaths in childbed from the eighteenth century to 1935' *Medical History* 30, pp. 1–41.

Loudon, I. (1988) 'Maternal mortality: 1880–1950. Some regional and international comparisons' *Social History of Medicine* 1, pp. 183–228.

McDowall, M. (1983) 'William Farr and the study of occupational mortality' *Population Trends* 31, pp. 12–14.

McKeown, T. (1976) *The Modern Rise of Population* (London).

McKeown, T. (1979) *Role of Medicine: Dream, Mirage or Nemesis* (Oxford).

McKeown, T. and Brown, R. G. (1955) 'Medical evidence related to English population changes in the eighteenth century' *Population Studies* 9, pp. 119–41.

McKeown, T. and Record, R. G. (1962) 'Reasons for the decline of mortality in England and Wales during the nineteenth century' *Population Studies* 16, pp. 94–122.

Malthus, T., Record, R. G. and Turner, R. D. (1975) 'An interpretation of the decline of mortality in England and Wales during the twentieth century' *Population Studies* 29, pp. 391–422.

Mercer, A. (1990) *Disease, Mortality and Population in Transition:*

Epidemiological-Demographic Change in England since the Eighteenth Century as part of a Global Phenomenon (Leicester).

Newsholme, A. (1889) *The Elements of Vital Statistics* (London).

Pelling, M. (1978) *Cholera, Fever and English Medicine, 1825–1865* (Oxford).

Pickstone, J. V. (1985) *Medicine and Industrial Society: a History of Development in Manchester and its Region, 1752–1946* (Manchester).

Reves, R. (1985) 'Declining fertility in England and Wales as a major cause of the twentieth century decline in mortality: the role of changing family size and age structure in infectious disease mortality in infancy' *American Journal of Epidemiology* 122, pp. 112–26.

Riley, J. C. (1989) *Sickness. Recovery and Death: A History and Forecast of Ill Health* (London).

Smith, F. B. (1979) *The People's Health, 1830–1910* (London).

Smith, F. B. (1988) *The Retreat of Tuberculosis, 1850–1950* London).

Szreter, S. R. S. (1988) 'The importance of social intervention in Britain's mortality decline c.1850–1914: a re-interpretation of the role of public health' *Social History of Medicine* 1, pp. 1–37.

Watterson, P. A. (1986) 'Role of the environment in the decline of infant mortality: an analysis of the 1911 Census of England and Wales' *Journal of Biosocial Science* 18, pp. 457–70.

Watterson, P. A. (1988) 'Infant mortality by father's occupation from the 1911 Census of England and Wales' *Demography* 25, pp. 289–306.

Williamson, J. G. (1982) 'Was the industrial revolution worth it? Disamenities and death in 19th century British towns' *Explorations in Economic History* 19, pp. 221–45.

Williamson, J. G. (1984) 'British mortality and the value of life, 1781–1931' *Population Studies* 38, pp. 157–72.

Williamson, J. G. (1990) *Coping with City Growth During the British Industrial Revolution* (Cambridge).

Wohl, A. S. (1983) *Endangered Lives: Public Health in Victorian Britain* (London).

Woods, R. I. (1985) 'The effects of population redistribution on the level of mortality in nineteenth-century England and

Wales' *Journal of Economic History* 45, pp. 645–51.

Woods, R. I. (1991) 'Public health via hygiene and sanitation: the urban environment in the late nineteenth and early twentieth centuries' in R. S. Schofield, D. Reher and A. Bideau (eds) *The Great Mortality Decline: A Reassessment of the European Experience* (Oxford), pp. 232–47.

Woods, R. I. and Hinde, P. R. A. (1987) 'Mortality in Victorian England: models and patterns' *Journal of Interdisciplinary History* 18, pp. 27–54.

Woods, R. I., Watterson, P. A. and Woodward, J. H. (1988–89) 'The causes of rapid infant mortality decline in England and Wales, 1861–1921. Parts I and II' *Population Studies* 42, pp. 343–66 and 43, pp. 113–32.

Woods, R. I. and Woodward, J. H. (eds) (1984) *Urban Disease and Mortality in Nineteenth Century England* (London).

Chapter 7 – 1911

Flinn, M. W. (1970) *British Population Growth, 1700–1850* (London).

Wrigley, E. A. (1983b) 'The growth of population in eighteenth-century England: a conundrum resolved' *Past and Present* 98, pp. 121–50.

Index